Hope for the Weary Mom

DEVOTIONAL

STACEY THACKER

BROOKE MCGLOTHLIN

HARVEST HOUSE PUBLISHERS
EUGENE, OREGON

Cover by Knail, Salem, Oregon

Published with the association of MacGregor Literary, Inc.

HOPE FOR THE WEARY MOM DEVOTIONAL
Copyright © 2015 Stacey Thacker and Brooke McGlothlin
Published by Harvest House Publishers
Eugene, Oregon 97402
www.harvesthousepublishers.com

Library of Congress Cataloging-in-Publication Data
    Thacker, Stacey, 1971-
    Hope for the weary mom devotional / Stacey Thacker and Brooke McGlothlin.
        pages cm
    ISBN 978-0-7369-6136-3 (pbk.)
    ISBN 978-0-7369-6137-0 (eBook)
    1. Mothers—Prayers and devotions. 2. Mothers—Religious life. 3. Motherhood—Religious aspects—Christianity. I. McGlothlin, Brooke, 1978- II. Title.
    BV4529.18.T445 2015
    242'.6431—dc23

                                                                        2015017108

Printed in the United States of America

            15 16 17 18 19 20 21 22 23 / BP-JH / 10 9 8 7 6 5 4 3 2 1

Contents

Acknowledgments

Stacey

Mike: Thank you for all you've done to make my dreams come true. You called me "writer" before anyone else. But then again, of course you did. Love you always.

My Girls: I am so blessed to be your mom. Thanks for loving me well and cheering me on.

Mom: Thank you for teaching me to cherish God's Word early in the morning.

Dad: I miss you every day. See you soon.

My "Fr" editors—Robin, Angie, Krystal, Emily, and Tanya: Thank you for taking the time to read rough words and encourage me. I owe you all a coffee date. My treat.

Brooke: I am grateful for your commitment to God's Word. You bless me every day, friend. Honored to be on this journey with you.

Chip: Thank you for believing in "Hope" and finding the perfect home for it. I am truly grateful for your support and hard work.

Kathleen and the Harvest House Publishers team: Thank you for saying yes and giving us a chance to reach even more moms with "Hope." It has been an honor partnering with you!

Jesus: May you be glorified through this humble offering and touch every heart who reads it.

Brooke

Writing a book is hard. Homeschooling, managing a business, feeding a family, and writing a book all at the same time is even harder. I would never have been able to do this without the support of my family and friends.

Cory: Thank you for just doing. For cleaning, washing, bathing, feeding, teaching, and all of the other things you did so I could have time to write. You're a gift to me.

Boys: You're the reason for this book, but even on the hardest days I'm still so very thankful that I get to be your mama. Thank you for keeping me desperate for Jesus, and for always giving me big, squishy boy hugs when I need them. You're my favorite boys in the world!

Mom and Dad: You've always believed in my dreams. Now, as an adult, I can clearly see that you've not only believed in my dreams, but sacrificed for them as well. I can only hope to love my children so well. Thank you for cutting your trip to Florida short to come home so I could have time to finish this book. I couldn't have done it without you.

Jamie and Meggen: Thank you so much for cheering me on, encouraging me to keep going, and for the way you have served me throughout the last difficult season of my life. I won't forget.

Kristin: You listened to the Lord. Thank you.

Stacey: I can't imagine writing this book with anyone else. If I had to be "stuck" with someone, I'm sure glad it was you! I'm so grateful for your words of advice and encouragement, both in this book and in my life.

Chip MacGregor: You believed in us and in the need to keep reaching out to weary moms. Thank you for catching the vision and for championing it for us in ways that went above and beyond the call of duty. We're so grateful for you.

The Hope for the Weary Mom launch team: No words really cut it. Thank you for your faithful prayers, feedback, and encouragement to get this message out. You are grace to us.

My Jesus: You're enough.

Introduction

Why...

The law of the LORD is perfect, reviving the soul; the testimony of the LORD is sure, making wise the simple.

PSALM 19:7

Brooke and I arrived early for our workshop at the conference. We planned it that way because we wanted to set up the room before we spoke. As it turned out, the conference was running a few minutes behind schedule. This was a blessing for us because we were wrestling with both our PowerPoint presentation and our nerves. We needed to settle each down to a manageable level. Brooke suggested we pray and I thought it was a fabulous idea.

We exhaled long and deep and we inhaled the peace only Jesus could give to two weary moms. I prayed first, and when I looked up to Brooke I realized she was walking among the chairs and touching each one of the sixty or so sitting empty. My heart bent beneath the weight of what we were about to speak.

"Lord, come," I whispered.

But what if the moms don't show up? I thought. I knew with so many workshops to choose from it was a possibility no one would choose ours. We finished committing our time to the Lord and filled our glasses with fresh water. We worked on waiting patiently.

Now fifteen minutes behind schedule, a few moms trickled into the room. We chatted with some we knew and introduced ourselves to others we had not met yet. We talked about what time to officially start the session when a few more moms came in and filled the remaining seats. Minutes later they filled the back of the room. More moms came in and sat in the aisle while others took a seat on the floor in the front. And they just kept coming in the room. They squeezed in tight and sat anywhere they could find space. This meant a few moms were sitting in a closet and others sat in the doorway and out into the hallway. Somebody grabbed chairs from a lounge nearby. I looked at Brooke and she stared back in amazement at me. We began our session twenty minutes late and had about two feet of room to speak from our podium because so many moms were crowded in to hear.

What we saw at that conference were moms hungry for hope. We see the same thing every other place we share our stories. Hope casts a net wide, and on this day, like so many others, we all just wanted to swim in it in the places we needed it most.

Toward the end of our session we talked about things we love most. Brooke cracked her heart wide open about prayer. I could have listened for hours because she fires up fiercely when she does. And then it was my turn to talk about how God uses his Word to stir our hearts with hope.

Later, we asked for questions and one brave mom raised her hand. She said, "How do I do that? I don't know where to look in my Bible for hope." We gave her a few ideas, but after the session Brooke and I looked at each other. One of us said, "I can't wait for the day we can hand her a book that feels a lot like *Hope for the Weary Mom* and looks a lot like truth." We dreamed of a book for moms that would point them right to Jesus—our source of hope. Something they could read in the morning or during naptime or while they were in the car line at school. It would be a devotional packed with forty truths that would encourage their mama hearts. It might be something they read every day or during seasons that were particularly hard on them. It would be something they could easily give to a friend as a gift.

This is the book you now hold in your hand. We have prayed about it. We have written it for you. We believe these forty truths will breathe new life into your soul. Why? Because Jesus has done that very thing for us as we have written it. We chose these truths and these verses because they mean something to us. We have memorized many of them. We have fallen to our knees and prayed them back to Jesus on our toughest days. We believe this is a great place for you to start getting to know the God who not only loves you most, but is willing to meet you right where you are—in the messy places of motherhood.

With hope,
Stacey & Brooke

How to Use this Book

When Stacey and I first thought about putting together a devotional for weary moms, we knew it needed to have two main purposes. First, to make you feel seen, loved, and understood. Not just by us (although we do), but by the God who loves you more than you can fathom. Second, to provide 40 truths you need to trust God in and with your mess.

We sat in sunny Florida (where Stacey gets to live) on the campus of Wycliffe Bible Translators with our Bibles, coffee, and maybe a few red Twizzlers in front of us, and asked the Lord what you needed to hear. What were the main things you needed to know from his Word to keep putting one foot in front of the other? What truths would give you a sure foundation, setting you up for success not just as a mom, but as a daughter of God?

The beauty of what we were doing didn't escape us. We were sitting in an apartment owned by the world's largest Bible translation ministry where missionaries come on furlough after giving of themselves to bring the Word of God to people in their own heart language. They served so that others could know the life-changing freedom found in Scripture. We were laboring for a similar kind of freedom—to bring real, lasting, soul-changing hope in a language weary moms could understand.

The book you have in front of you represents what we feel he showed us that day as we brainstormed.

You might be wondering how to use it. There's really no wrong way to get into the Word of God or this book. We've set it up so each of the 40 devotional chapters represent an emotion or circumstance most weary moms have experienced at some point in their lives. You may find that certain chapters speak to you on certain days better than others, and that's okay.

Here are some suggestions for a reading plan. Pick one that suits you during this season of your life, or feel free to come up with a completely different plan. Just get in there and start reading!

1. If you're a "from A to Z" person, start with chapter 1 and move throughout the book reading one devotion per day for 40 days. I've read it takes about 21 days to start a new habit. Our prayer is that by the time you finish the devotional, you'll be hungry for more!

2. If you have a particular need right now, look in the table of contents and pick the chapter title that speaks most closely to what you're going through. Each chapter is designed to both build on the one before and stand alone, so feel free to skip around as your emotions and circumstances lead you.

3. We highly recommend gathering together with a group of like-minded weary moms to do this devotional study together. It's been said that you should never drink (ahem…coffee!) alone, and we find the same advice applies to motherhood. We're stronger together, and in groups, can encourage each other toward Jesus. But…

4. If you're just too busy to join a group right now, the book can also serve as your personal daily devotion or quiet time. Stacey and I both choose to have our time

with Jesus early in the morning. We just find that it sets the tone for the rest of the day. But if you're the mom of very little ones, don't feel any pressure to get up early. God sees you and will bless any effort you give him. Have your quiet time before bed, while your littles nap, or some other creative alternative. The only thing that matters is *that* you do it, not *when* you do it.

5. Finally, our hearts were to create a resource you could come back to over and over. After you've finished this book, put it on your shelf and pull it out again and again, letting the truths in its pages fill your hearts and homes with hope.

Choose hope!
Brooke

He Is Good

*It is written, "Man shall not live by bread alone, but
by every word that comes from the mouth of God."*
M<small>ATTHEW</small> 4:4

Brooke

My husband walked up the stairs from the basement, shoulders slumped, brow creased, and wearing a heaviness in his heart that reeked of hopelessness.

The list of things in our home that were broken during that time was long—dishwasher, lawnmower, siding on our house—all in need of immediate repair. And now...

"The dryer is broken," he said, "and I can't even have someone come look at it because the basement is such a disaster. I'll have to spend the whole night cleaning after I get home from work so we can get it fixed. Even if I can figure it out I have no idea how we'll pay for it."

He kissed me on the forehead and walked out the door, leaving me with an open mouth and a hurting heart. I knew what our bank account said about the situation—it said, "Not enough to fix all the things," and "Where will the money come from?" and "Well, maybe if you don't eat this month..."

Paralyzed by financial fear, I closed my eyes and did the only thing I knew to do. As big, warm tears ran down my cheeks, I forced myself to pray and ask God to provide. I told him I knew he could, and wanted to believe he would, but I knew in my heart I was going to need help to keep faith in his goodness.

My husband works hard to provide for our family, but because we've chosen for me to be a stay-at-home mom, finances can sometimes be tight. We always have enough to eat and enough clothing to wear, but three large, necessary appliances breaking down in the same week is enough to make anyone question whether or not God is paying attention. I knew my husband was feeling the crushing weight of our finances just as much, if not more, than I was, and that that day, more than anything else, he needed me to give him hope.

But how could I give my husband hope when I was fighting so hard for it myself?

I walked downstairs and surveyed the mess before me. The laundry pile resembled the trash heap on Fraggle Rock (remember that show?)—totally out of control. Stacks of trash meant for the dumpster needed to be sorted. Mounds of toys, clothing, and other household items we didn't use anymore needed to be trashed or taken to Goodwill.

I wanted to tuck tail and run, but the basement was calling my name—or rather God was calling my name. It was time to get to work. I sensed that there was hope to be found in the midst of that terrible mess.

I got ready to head into the abyss, but I needed to take our dogs out before I took my shovel down to dig in. It was a hot day, and I was impatiently waiting for our labs to do their business when the second wave of financial fear hit me. I began to sweat more than what the weather called for and found it hard to catch my breath. The words *It's never going to get better* rang in my head and threatened to take me right under.

So I prayed again, "Lord, give me faith to believe that your heart for me is good enough to take care of our needs. I know you're good, but I need help to believe you're going to be good to me in this situation. I do believe, Lord. Help my unbelief."

Taking deep breaths, I exhaled the words, "I will not fear, for God is with me," over and over until my heart slowed back down and my breathing was under control.

That day, I cleaned our entire basement. When my husband came home from work, he cried. Turns out setting my needs aside for the day communicated to him that his needs were important to me, and that gave him hope to believe God was moving in our family and could move in our finances. My service blessed my husband's heart.

I continued to battle bouts of financial fear all day long. It caught me while dusting, while walking my clean laundry over to the neighbor's house to use her dryer, and while asking a friend to cover me in prayer.

But I battled fear with the hope that God is good.

When he was being tempted by Satan in the desert, Jesus fought—and found victory—with the Word of God. "It is written," he said. Jesus countered every temptation Satan threw his way with the truth written in what we now call the Old Testament, and you and I can do the same thing.

I survived that desperate time because of God's Word. You can too.

Next time you're faced with the fear that God won't be good to you in a certain situation, remind yourself of what you know to be true. I know God is good because I've tasted and seen his goodness before. I believe his Word is true because I've seen him prove it over and over again. I know I don't have to be afraid because really, and truly, God is with me.

And in the very moment of fear—the very moment when I feel my most vulnerable, wondering if God will pull through and be good to me one more time—I can say *No!* to my temptation to fear and *Yes!* to God's truth instead, allowing his perspective to flood mine, pushing fear away with it.

This is the freedom we have in Christ. This is the power of Christ at work in us. This is the hope that God is, and always will be, good.

Pray with me?

> Lord, help me believe in your Word. Help me to trust what I hear you say over what I hear from the world, especially when I'm in the storms of life, where your voice seems small. Be with me today, so close, and help me follow after you even when it's hard. In Jesus's name, amen.

Going Deeper

- What recent situation has left you feeling that God isn't good?

- Take a moment to look through the Bible, maybe with a concordance nearby, and see if you can find a verse that speaks to your situation. Claim it as yours. Memorize it. Speak it to your own heart whenever you're tempted to lose faith.

- Make a post-it note of this verse and stick it somewhere you'll see it multiple times a day.

∞∞∞∞∞∞∞∞∞∞∞∞∞∞∞∞∞∞∞∞∞∞∞∞∞∞∞∞∞∞

In the very moment of fear—the very moment when
I feel my most vulnerable, wondering if God will pull
through and be good to me one more time—I can say
No! to my temptation to fear and *Yes!* to God's truth
instead, allowing his perspective to flood mine, pushing
fear away with it.

∞∞∞∞∞∞∞∞∞∞∞∞∞∞∞∞∞∞∞∞∞∞∞∞∞∞∞∞∞∞

He Cares

*Look at the lilies and how they grow. They don't work
or make their clothing, yet Solomon in all his glory
was not dressed as beautifully as they are. And if God
cares so wonderfully for flowers that are here today
and thrown into the fire tomorrow, he will certainly
care for you. Why do you have so little faith?*

LUKE 12:27-28 NLT

Stacey

I'll admit it. I was stressed. I was struggling and feeling a little unnoticed by God, who seemed to be silent and busy caring for much bigger, more pressing needs than mine. So I asked him for a sign. I wasn't testing him to prove who he was. I simply longed for evidence of his personal care and attention in my small life. My prayer request was that he let me see a mother deer and her fawn on the way to work one morning.

Each morning my husband and I drove to work through a wildlife nature preserve, so this wasn't an outrageous request. I had seen deer multiple times. But I had not seen a doe and her fawn in particular. I was filled with expectation, but as we drove we saw nothing. I was embarrassed by my own behavior. I felt a little bit like a child who had asked for candy before dinner. I honestly thought it was my request that was misguided, not God's lack of care for my prayer.

We worked in a Christian office and regularly had staff devotions. As we started our time together that morning my boss, Paul, began to tell about his ride into work that morning. He lived in town a few miles away from our office. "I saw the most amazing thing today in a busy intersection. A baby deer was lying down in the middle of the street and its mother was protecting it. Every car stopped and waited as the mother nudged and encouraged the baby out of harm's way."

I nearly fell out of my chair. God spoke directly to my heart as Paul finished his story. "Is there anything too hard for me? I could have shown you a mother deer and her fawn in the wildlife preserve. But instead, I chose to show you I work in ways you sometimes cannot see. My care for you is just like this mother and her baby. I will always be here, nudging you out of harm's way, encouraging your heart in the most extravagant ways."

I didn't really need to ask God to show me he cares for me. He already wrote about it in great detail in his Word. For example, the Bible tells a story of how one day a large crowd gathered around Jesus. They were pressing in, broken, needy, and listening to his words. He turned to his disciples, whom he called "dear friends," and reminded them "not to worry about everyday life—whether you have enough food to eat or enough clothes to wear. For life is more than food, and your body more than clothing" (Luke 12:22-23 NLT). And then he pointed to the nearby field and urged them to consider God's creation and its effortless beauty. "Do you see the flowers sweating over it? God is a gardener who cares for their needs. He cares for the simple flowers of the field. Will he do any less for you?"

I think we moms are like the disciples. Our crowd is pressing in and they are needy. They are looking at us to meet their daily needs. The whole time we are looking at Jesus, saying, "Do you care that I'm in over my head, Lord?"

In the most gentle way, he says, "Look at the flowers. Look at the birds. I care for them and I am going to take care of you, because you mean so much more to me." He is lifting our eyes to see over and beyond our desperate situation. He points to the sky when we take our walk in the evening. He directs our attention to a bird singing in the tree while we are making dinner. He is dropping little hints all day long that he is always caring for us as we are caring for others.

I asked God to show me the mother deer and her baby many years ago. It was long before I became a mom. God was sweet to indulge me in my request because he is full of grace and ever so patient. He is a personal and loving God—always.

Not too long ago I was drinking my coffee and staring out the window. We live in town but have a small patch of woods behind our home. I was quietly telling the Lord I was already weary. I needed to sense his care for me as I cared for my girls. Can you guess what walked by my window? This time, I got to see the mother deer and her fawn with my own eyes. This pair had taken up residence in that little patch of woods. For several weeks, during some of my hardest mom days, they would walk across my backyard. And God would say, "Why do you have so little faith? I care for you like this. I am here, and nothing is too hard for me."

Pray with me?

> Lord, open my eyes to see your care for my heart. May I see you loving me every day as I love and serve my own family. Thank you for the sweet truth that nothing is too hard for you. In Jesus's name, amen.

Going Deeper

- How has God shown you personally he cares for you?
- Can you trust him with your everyday life right now?

<hr>

If we are going to make it every day as moms,
we need to consider his care on days when
we would rather despair.

He Sees You

*For the eyes of the LORD range throughout
the earth to strengthen those whose
hearts are fully committed to him.*

2 CHRONICLES 16:9 NIV

Stacey

We are the ones who wake up early to make lunches for school. We wash dishes until well past midnight and fold laundry without ceasing. We are boo-boo kissers, shoe putter-on-ers, and seatbelt checkers. We are in constant motion all day long. And in the middle of the night when our babies cry out for milk or our children have a bad dream, we are the ones who leap out of bed at their first sound of need. We are moms. This is what we do.

So much of our lives are spent serving in the small ways and, when added up, matter in life-sized proportions. But most days our acts of service happen without reward or recognition from others. We move throughout our busy days as the hidden hands and feet of Jesus in the lives of our people. We love them, but we sometimes find ourselves wondering, "Does anyone at all notice I am here?" Unsung and unseen, we can begin to believe life behind our front door is small and doesn't matter one bit.

Nothing could be further from the truth.

Years ago God put his finger on 2 Chronicles 16:9 for me. I had no idea it was there, waiting for me in his Word. When I found it, I quickly memorized it because I knew it was a verse I would go back to time and time again. I have looked it up hundreds of times to make sure I have it right and to see for myself it is actually still there. This is a powerful truth.

See, the first lie from the enemy I am prone to believe is that *I am alone and no one truly sees me*. I am easily convinced God has no idea about my state of affairs. If I camp out in this feeling for too long, I find myself taking matters into my own hands and trying to fix my life according to my best efforts. I fail miserably, and the enemy is pleased with himself for getting me to easily believe a familiar falsehood. He doesn't have any new tricks up his sleeve and he knows this one has worked before. So he often returns to it in my life.

Until, that is, I found a truth to destroy that lie. My God is not unaware. He is perched on his throne and he is looking for those whose hearts are completely his. Since my heart is his home, this includes me. He is looking for you too. Why? Because he desires to show himself strong in our lives. He wants to sustain and secure us. We are not unseen. He has the power to strengthen us for the holy calling placed on our lives—mothering. Especially on our most weary-filled days.

Jesus was an expert at seeing too. He saw children pushing in to be near him, so he pulled them onto his lap. He saw a sinful woman caught in adultery and stepped in to save her. He saw Zacchaeus trying to see him and called him down to dinner. He saw Martha in the kitchen and Mary at his feet. He saw a thief when he was dying on the cross. Each time he saw them and he offered exactly what they needed to move one step further. He offered himself.

God sees. He always has. Jesus showed us what seeing looked like in everyday life. We don't have to be on a stage for God to notice our need. We can be assured he sees us when we think no one knows or we don't want anyone to know and have firmly hidden ourselves at the nearest Starbucks. Yeah, he goes there, too. And it is not for the peppermint white mocha. It is for the girl drinking it. He wants to strengthen and comfort her weary mama heart.

Pray with me?

> Lord, thank you for seeing me and constantly support-ing me. My heart and my life are completely yours, Jesus. Weariness overwhelms me some days, and I am prone to believe I am alone. Jesus, thank you for the truth found in your Word that reminds me of truth. You see me every minute of every day. In Jesus's name, amen.

Going Deeper

- When do you feel unseen?
- How does your heart respond to the truth God not only sees you, but he is fervently searching for your heart so he can strengthen you?

Unsung and unseen, we can begin to believe life behind our front door is small and doesn't matter one bit. Nothing could be further from the truth.

He Can Take Your Truth

*Come, see a man who told me all that I
ever did. Can this be the Christ?*

JOHN 4:25

Brooke

I sat in the late evening sun on the front porch of our home, head in hands, tears streaming down my face, rendered speechless by the realization that I didn't have what it took to be the kind of mom I wanted to be.

Before having kids, I'd never really failed at anything. Oh sure, I had been through failed relationships, had come close to failing a test here and there, and had failed to live up to my own expectations from time to time, but never the big things. Every goal I set for myself I achieved. But as a mom—the one thing I really wanted to get right in life—I was failing.

I wanted everyone to believe that I was capable of handling the two beautiful boys God gave me, but I wasn't.

I wanted everyone to believe I could juggle work, kids, husband, home, and church with ease, but I couldn't.

I wanted everyone to believe that crying babies, nursing problems, shift work, and the Terrible Twos weren't too much for me all at once, but they were.

And what I wanted everyone to believe—that I was a confident, capable, smart, fully independent woman—was keeping me from admitting the truth. I really didn't have what it took. When I tried harder, things got worse. When I prayed more, I felt weak. When I tried to hide what was really going on in our lives, I felt ashamed, and when God didn't come down and make it all better like I wanted him to, I got mad.

I kept the curtains to our home closed most of the time during those days, and I avoided situations where my shame could be revealed, because if I didn't...

One day when my husband was working, I tried attending his great-aunt's ninetieth birthday party with the boys. They were just four and two at the time. I left nearly hyperventilating with panic and fear as I carried them both out of the party, one under each arm, kicking and screaming. I wasn't upset because they wouldn't obey (okay, maybe I was a little). I was upset because everyone I loved saw the ugly truth of my life up close and personal. I had two little boys I couldn't control. I had failed.

When I think about coming face-to-face with the truth, I think of the woman at the well. She knew the weight of failure. Much like the weight of the water jug she carried in the heat of the day, her failures hung about her shoulders, pulling her down and reminding her who she was. An adulterer. Married five times and living with a man not her husband. She went to the well at the hottest part of the day to avoid the stares of the people who had watched her fail over and over and over again.

I kind of did the same thing.

Unable to shoulder the weight of what I assumed others thought of me because of my over-the-top boys, I avoided people altogether. I skipped communion on the Sundays my husband worked because I knew I would fail. I avoided birthday parties because their already hyped-up atmosphere was like rocket fuel, causing my boys to be even more energetic—and harder to handle—than normal, and I never, ever told anyone what I was experiencing. I just cried in my bed at night and awoke to the chaos again the next morning. It was a redundant, monotonous life. Failing day in and day out at the thing I most wanted to do well.

And then it all changed.

I sat on the porch that day and asked God if he knew who he was dealing with. I mean, really, did he see what was going on in our home? Did he know how many times I had tried and failed? Did he understand how painful my life had become?

His reply? "Yes, I do." Of course he does. He can take our truth because he makes our truth.

The Samaritan woman at the well? She thought that day at the well would be just like any other in her redundant, monotonous life too. That is, until she met Jesus.

In a world where Jews and Samaritans didn't mix, Jesus saw into her heart and gave her a drink of living water. With a few words from the one who changes everything, she went from hiding her failures to bursting forth into praise and shouting, "Come, see a man who told me all that I ever did. Can this be the Christ?" (John 4:29).

Shedding the weight of her shame, she came out of hiding that day. She no longer cared to hide her sin. No...now she was proclaiming it! Giving glory to the one who knew her, loved her, changed her, redeemed her, and in her excitement she ran to tell everyone else.

I'm not suggesting that you need to walk up to perfect strangers and tell them all about your failures as a mom, but I am suggesting that Jesus can handle the ugly truth of your situation, regardless of what it might be.

Not only can he handle it, he can get down in it with you and change it. How? By changing you.

As you open your heart to him, get to know his Word, tell the truth about what's happening in your home, and ask for help from others around you, he'll meet you in your mess and make you more like him. That, my friend, changes the whole equation.

Pray with me?

> Lord, I confess sometimes my truth seems too big. I'm shamed by the things I can't control and want to hide so no one knows. Help me step out from behind the curtain today. Assure me, right this moment, that you'll never leave me or forsake me, and help me remember that what you think of me is always much more important than the opinions of anyone else. In Jesus's name, amen.

Going Deeper

- Take a moment to admit it. You don't have what it takes to be the kind of mom you want to be. I know it's a hard thing to admit, but you'll feel so much freedom in just acknowledging the truth.

- Next, pray and ask the Lord to show you how to pull back the curtains of your life and to give you the strength you need to tell the truth to at least one friend. If you don't have a friend you can share with, ask the Lord to bring you one.

∞∞∞∞∞∞∞∞∞∞∞∞∞∞∞∞∞∞∞∞∞∞∞∞∞∞∞∞∞∞∞

He can take our truth because he makes our truth.

∞∞∞∞∞∞∞∞∞∞∞∞∞∞∞∞∞∞∞∞∞∞∞∞∞∞∞∞∞∞∞

He Chose You

God chose us to be in a relationship with Him
even before He laid out plans for this world; He
wanted us to live holy lives characterized by
love, free from sin, *and blameless before Him.*

EPHESIANS 1:4 THE VOICE

Stacey

$\mathscr{I}$ wish we were sitting together at a coffee shop right now. I
would have a vanilla latte with whipped topping and a chocolate muffin the size of a softball sitting in front of me. I would take
a sip and look you square in the eye and say, "I have a family secret
I want to tell you."

I would lean across the table and you would too because secrets
are always whispered. After a pregnant pause I would say, "You are
chosen. Selected. And it has been this way since before God spoke
the world into being. Your being his daughter has always been part
of his plan. You were wanted then, and you are wanted now."

Would you believe me? Would you sit back, close your eyes, and receive it? Would it move your heart and cause tears to run down your cheeks?

It does me too.

See, I know what it feels like to be passed by and ignored. My first memory of being passed by was in the eighth grade. I was one of the only girls not to have a date to our eighth grade dance. I really wanted one particular boy to ask me. But he chose someone else. I thought about staying home that night and watching a movie instead, but my mom encouraged me to pick out a pretty dress and go anyhow. She bought me a pink corsage and I cried when she pinned it on me.

Undesirable is a deeply felt emotion.

The dance was fine and for the most part the girls stayed on one side and their "dates" on the other. During the slow songs I sat alone and tried to be invisible. I was the definition of wallflower. This went on all night until the final song when I felt a tap on my shoulder. See, my older brother, a senior in high school, was a DJ for the dance that night. When I looked up, I saw him standing in front of me. He said, "Come on, sis, let's dance." He gave me little choice before he grabbed my hand and planted me in the middle of the floor. We danced the last couple of songs and every eighth grader was staring at us.

You should know a couple of things: First, my brother was pretty cute. Second, he could really dance. Third, most of the kids did not know he was my brother. I was the envy of every girl because the cute DJ had asked the wallflower to dance. The fact that he *was* my brother only made it sweeter for me. It helped me see that eighth grade would not last forever and there was always a reason to dance.

It is easy to fade into the background of your life as mom and play the wallflower. We are needed by our families every day, but are we desirable and chosen? The answer in Christ is a resounding *yes*!

He handpicked you and every day he desires to sweep you up in a dance of celebration. Here is the good news: It is not because of what you do or how you look or how you dress. Your merits are found in who he is. God sees you as positively blameless because Jesus is all that on your behalf. So, my dear sweet friend, you don't have to win his grace. You don't have to perform for it. It is part of your family legacy. Warren Weirsbe says, "We cannot fully explain it but we can fully enjoy it. Do not try to explain away the mystery of grace."*

This mysterious grace has me thinking. What if we lived, loved, free from sin, and utterly blameless every day? What if we put on our happy dress and pinned a pink flower in our hair especially on the days we *felt* pretty undesirable? I think our kids would catch us dancing in the kitchen more often. And we would be smiling through tears.

Pray with me?

> Today I choose, Lord, to celebrate the grace I have in Jesus Christ as your daughter. Please keep whispering over my life: *chosen, blameless,* and *free*. I will live it and dance with you because of it. In Jesus's name, amen.

Going Deeper

What could this truth change in your day-to-day life if you believed it by faith?

∞∞∞∞∞∞∞∞∞∞∞∞∞∞∞∞∞∞∞∞∞∞∞∞∞∞∞∞∞∞∞∞

Christ handpicked you and every day he desires to
sweep you up in a dance of celebration.

∞∞∞∞∞∞∞∞∞∞∞∞∞∞∞∞∞∞∞∞∞∞∞∞∞∞∞∞∞∞∞∞

---

* Warren Wiersbe, *Expository Outlines on the New Testament* (Colorado Springs, CO; David C. Cook, 1992), 538.

He Gives You Peace

Peace I leave with you; my peace I give to you. Not
as the world gives do I give to you. Let not your
hearts be troubled, neither let them be afraid.

JOHN 14:27

Brooke

One of my favorite childhood meals was brown beans and rice
smothered in ketchup.

I know it sounds gross, but it's delicious. Truly. My older brother
recently shared some of his precious soaked overnight, cooked-all-
day beans (no can, y'all, they were amazing!), and as I stirred the rice
to go with them, it occurred to me that it had probably been 15 years
since I had last eaten this dish.

So I ate it slowly. And I didn't share.

As I closed my mouth around each bite, my eyes closed to taste
buds remembering how much I loved it as a child. A feeling of
warmth and peace snuck into my heart, radiating out through the
rest of my body. I actually felt myself relax into a place of peace right

there at the dinner table as I let go of the things of the world and just enjoyed one simple bite of my childhood.

James 1:17 tells us that every good and perfect gift is from above. It might be in the form of a good dish of beans and rice with ketchup, or it might be a simple reminder that we're not alone. Whatever it is, I'm convinced that God is the one who gives it.

But do we always see it?

John 14:27 assures us that followers of Jesus will be given peace. But do you see what else is tucked into that small verse believers have been quoting for centuries? There are two things I'd love for you to see.

1. Peace isn't the absence of pain. It's the presence and promise of God.

Don't we wish it was? Don't we wish we could just snap our fingers and make all the hard things of life go away? On my difficult days I sometimes wish for that kind of peace.

The world defines peace as being free from disturbances, and I get it. It's absolutely, 100 percent easier for me to find peace when I'm alone in a quiet house with no one tugging on me and calling me "Mommy." But as a believer, I can also find peace in the midst of trying circumstances, tantrums, disagreements, and the general challenges of life.

My peace has nothing to do with what's happening around me. It has to do with a loving God who has promised to never leave me. Peace happens when the goodness of God intersects the craziness of life. If you can find peace while supper is burning on the stove, the fifth grader needs help with homework, and you're tidying up the house before hubby comes home, you can find it anywhere. That's the difference between peace the world gives and peace the Father gives. His peace is with us always as we remember his promises to be good.

2. Peace is faith in action.

God says he gives us peace, but are we choosing it? I know it seems hard in the midst of the chaos, but the last part of John 14:27 says, "*Let* not your hearts be troubled, neither *let* them be afraid" (emphasis mine). This implies that while God has left us peace to help weather the storms of life, we have to exercise faith to actually live it.

For me, this looks like calling my husband at work to ask for prayer in the midst of a trying day. It looks like turning on worship music and blaring it into my home and heart, drowning out the voice of the enemy as he attempts to lead me astray. It means praying before entering situations I know are chaotic and asking the Lord to meet me there. It means pausing in the middle of a big mess of a day and inviting the Lord to change my perspective.

Sometimes, it means just speaking the truth to myself over and over until I believe it again—a deep breath that relaxes my body and gives my heart a chance to see through the clutter.

Peace is the hard-won right of the wearied Christian, a fight to receive what God has gladly given.

Pray with me?

> Father, thank you for not leaving us stranded with no means of respite in this difficult world. Today, we're putting our faith in your promise to be with us no matter what. Help us to believe it even when we can't see it. Let the truth of your word resonate in our hearts and grant us peace. In Jesus's name, amen.

Going Deeper

- What are some of your biggest distractions in life? How do they keep you from experiencing peace?

- When I really need peace, I always default to piano

music. What music brings you peace? We've created a playlist for you with some of our favorite peaceful worship music. Feel free to download it at www.hopeforthe wearymom.com/freebies!

∞∞∞∞∞∞∞∞∞∞∞∞∞∞∞∞∞∞∞∞∞∞∞∞∞

Peace has nothing to do with what's happening around me. It has to do with a loving God who has promised to never leave me.

∞∞∞∞∞∞∞∞∞∞∞∞∞∞∞∞∞∞∞∞∞∞∞∞∞

He Never Leaves You

I will never leave you nor forsake you.

HEBREWS 13:5

Stacey

A few years ago I sat in our navy blue minivan with my husband beside me and our three-year-old daughter strapped in her car seat behind me. I was eight months pregnant with our second daughter and we were moving to a new town thousands of miles away. I watched it rain as we drove through the night, and somewhere near Atlanta I wondered what in the world the Lord was doing moving me so far away from the place I called home. I prayed the entire trip, and when we pulled in front of our new home I had a choice to make. Truthfully, I have never felt more alone in my life. Would I trust the one who uttered the promise of Hebrews 13:5 to show himself faithful in my life?

The richness of this promise is found in the original Greek language in which it was penned. We need to lay aside our English grammar rules and feel the full impact of its intended meaning. The writer wanted to make it very clear:

"I will never, never, leave you, I will never, never, never forsake you."

How clear? He used five negatives in this one sentence. What is the chance that God will leave you? Never. Never. What is the occasion he will forsake you? Never. Never. Never. Don't let the double and triple negatives get you all in a fuss. Let it put you in a place of absolute assurance that he will certainly not loosen his hold or utterly abandon you. The beauty of this promise found in the New Testament is it occurs several times in the Old Testament as well. It is a covenant promise spoken again and again throughout the ages to assure us God is in the business of holding fast to his children:

- He spoke it to the patriarchs of our faith (Genesis 28:15).

- He repeated it to the forgetful people of Judah (Deuteronomy 31:6)

- He declared it to warriors going into battle (Joshua 1:5).

- He spoke through kings and to their sons (1 Chronicles 28:20).

- For the rest of us who are poor and needy (Isaiah 41:17).

This promise is like a scarlet thread of hope that runs through God's Word and is bound to you as well. It is part of the covenant he delights in keeping. What does it mean for weary moms like you and me? I love how Charles Spurgeon puts it:

> To put everything in one, there is nothing you can want, there is nothing you can ask for, there is nothing you can need in time or in eternity, there is nothing living, nothing dying, there is nothing in this world, nothing in the next world, there is nothing now, nothing at the

resurrection-morning, nothing in heaven that is not contained in this text—"I will never leave thee; I will never forsake thee."*

It means everything. It means you can trust him. It means no matter who abandons you, God won't. It means even if you move a thousand miles away from home, he will move with you. You can't send him away with your anger or ask for something he can't deliver. He whispers it on Monday. He shouts it on Friday. You can't unglue him from his covenant commitment to you.

Never. Never. Never. Never. Never.

He said it. You can believe it.

Pray with me?

> Lord, it is a powerful promise to say you will never leave me. Thank you for this thread of hope that runs all the way through your word straight to my heart. In Jesus's name, amen.

Going Deeper

- Where and when are you most likely to feel like God will in some way abandon you?

- Today, no matter how you feel, can you choose to believe that he will never, never leave you?

◇◇◇◇◇◇◇◇◇◇◇◇◇◇◇◇◇◇◇◇◇◇◇◇◇◇◇◇◇◇◇◇◇◇◇◇◇◇◇

"I will never, never, leave you,
I will never, never, never forsake you."

◇◇◇◇◇◇◇◇◇◇◇◇◇◇◇◇◇◇◇◇◇◇◇◇◇◇◇◇◇◇◇◇◇◇◇◇◇◇◇

---

* Charles Spurgeon, "Never! Never! Never! Never! Never!" (sermon, Metropolitan Tabernacle, Newington, England, October 26, 1862).

He Heals

*Every branch in me that does not bear fruit he
takes away, and every branch that does bear
fruit he prunes, that it may bear more fruit.*

JOHN 15:2

Brooke

I wanted Jesus to heal my uncle.

I sat across from my husband at our favorite local pizza
dive with tears in my eyes and said, "I'm not ready for this." I knew
it was coming—could feel it in my bones and in my heart—a season of loss, stripping, laying bare, and eventual rebuilding. Somehow, I knew it was coming. Maybe that was the Lord's grace, but it
didn't make it easier.

A stripping it was.

I watched my uncle fight and lose his battle with pulmonary
fibrosis, his lungs hardening over time until he could barely breathe
at all...and over the course of several years, I prayed and hoped Jesus
would heal him.

It was my dad's other brother who actually started the cycle, passing away on my youngest son's first birthday. Ten months later, the one I'd thought would go first joined him. Then my grandfather, then my aunt, then my baby, then my grandmother. And I'd prayed Jesus would heal them all.

But he didn't. Or at least not here, and that's not what I prayed for. I wanted him to heal them here so I could enjoy more time with them, but that wasn't his plan.

Sometimes, it's hard to submit to God's plan.

As moms, we're convinced we know what's best for our kids—that our way really is the best way for them. We see their gifts, their talents, their possibility, and we sacrifice to help them reach the fullest *them* they can be. And then God doesn't always heal when we need him to, leaving us wondering why it all matters, and if any of it is worth it.

But he does do what he set out to do. He accomplishes what he came for in his timing. And friends, today, I want to help us not lose sight of the significance of that gift.

When Jesus walked among us, he healed many sick. Crowds brought their lame, blind, bleeding, leprous, dying friends and family to the Savior in hopes that just a mere touch of his garment would bring them peace. And it was peace Jesus came to give, but not just of the physical kind. Maybe not even primarily of the physical kind.

Jesus came to give life, but not just the living and breathing kind. Maybe not even primarily the living and breathing kind.

Jesus came to give hope, but not just hope to save our bodies. He came to give hope that could save our souls.

∞∞∞∞∞∞∞∞∞∞∞∞∞∞∞∞∞∞∞∞∞∞∞

Why do we seek him? Is it so he can perform for us, take care of all our needs, bind up our wounds, raise

our dead? He is that God. He sees us. But if we only
follow him because of what he does, there will come a
time when we feel like he doesn't. And then we must
choose if we will turn away or follow through the times
when life hurts too much because of who he is, not
what he does. —from *Hope for the Weary Mom*

⬦⬦⬦⬦⬦⬦⬦⬦⬦⬦⬦⬦⬦⬦⬦⬦⬦⬦⬦⬦⬦⬦⬦⬦⬦⬦⬦⬦

Friends, Jesus didn't come just to heal our bodies of sickness.
Occasionally, just because he loves us so much and because it brings
him the most glory, he heals our disease, but it's not the main reason
he came. He came to heal our souls.

Today, I want to ask you to take a good, hard look at why you're
following Jesus. Is it because of all he's done for you? Good: that's
wonderful, right, and true. But there's more. When the tough times
come, and they will, your ability to follow anyway will need to be
based on something deeper, and that can only be found in who he
is. Your love for him will need to sustain you even when you can't
see him at work in your life.

Thankfully, it's your experience of Jesus now, in the good times,
that will fuel your faith in the hard times. So if you're hanging out
in the sweet times, with blue skies all around and not a drop of rain
in sight, get in his Word. Get to know him NOW, and commit to
following him even when the going gets tough.

If you're already in the hard times, remember this: Painful though
it may be, allowing God to strip you of the things he can't use is always
best. Many years ago, when I was just a girl, my grandfather was in an
accident that left him with severe burns all over his body. The doctors
called the family in several times during the five months he was in the
burn unit at UVA, thinking he wasn't going to make it. He did, but
while there, he had to undergo the painful process of debridement.

Debridement is scraping away old, dead skin so the new skin can have room to grow and heal. Horror stories are told about how excruciatingly painful this process is, no matter how sedated the patients are. But unless it's done, the new skin can't do what it was designed to do.

So it is with you, my friend.

Unless God removes the things that don't bring him glory—the things that are dead, rotting, and preventing health—we'll never walk in the fullness of what we were designed by God to do. Yes, it hurts like the dickens. The process can be excruciating at times, leaving us crying out in pain no matter what we do to make it go away. But the end result is something more beautiful than we could ever have created on our own. New life. Beauty from ashes. And the ability to walk in the fullness of who we were created to be.

Pray with me?

> Lord, I don't always like the healing process. I'd much rather just blink my eyes and be done with it, skipping all the painful parts like repentance and confession. So that's my confession. I know you know my heart because you created it. Gently, and lovingly get me to the place I need to be so I can be the woman you created me to be. In Jesus's name, amen.

Going Deeper

- Are you in a season of debridement? What is God stripping away that you'd rather hold on to?

- Can you trust him enough to let it go, knowing that his plans for you—those lying just beneath the surface—are so much better?

∞∞∞∞∞∞∞∞∞∞∞∞∞∞∞∞∞∞∞∞∞∞∞∞∞∞∞∞∞∞∞

Jesus came to give hope, but not just hope to save our bodies. He came to give hope that could save our souls.

∞∞∞∞∞∞∞∞∞∞∞∞∞∞∞∞∞∞∞∞∞∞∞∞∞∞∞∞∞

He Fights for You

The LORD will fight for you; you need only to be still.
EXODUS 14:14 NIV

Brooke

$\mathcal{I}$ had a fight at obscene-thirty in the morning.

Maybe it was because I was alone in the hotel room and felt vulnerable lying there in the dark. Or maybe it was because I'd had my breath taken away by an insult two days before, and I was fighting to hear the word of God over the hurtful words of a "friend." Or maybe it was just that I held in my heart the weight of 120 women who had come to us for hope that weekend.

Whatever the reason, I was in a fight with the enemy of my soul at about 5:30 in the morning and I was determined to win.

I'd spent the day before telling mamas not to give up, to keep fighting for their children. I'd shared the story of how God told me my children needed someone to fight for them, and that he'd chosen that person to be me. It's a powerful story—I know it is because it's the one people mention to me most often, and one that God reminds me of every time I throw my hands up in the air and want to quit.

But there I was, lying in the bed, feeling the temptation to quit fighting. It was strong. I could taste the battle of it—good on one shoulder, evil on the other—and literally tossed and turned trying to drown out the voice of the enemy. I know him. He only comes to kill, steal, and destroy (John 10:10). He's not my friend (or yours) so listening to him is futile. But sometimes, it's hard to drown him out. Especially when he sucker punches you out of nowhere. That's how I felt that morning.

I've fought the fiery darts of the enemy for what seems like a life-time—fear of being hurt, fear of rejection, fear of failure. Fear has been a constant companion my entire life, and the enemy knows it. He's upped his attacks, gone for the jugular, hit me below the belt, and questioned my motives. But the difference between the woman I am now and the one I was ten years ago is *I know how to fight him.*

I don't always want to. That morning I *wanted* to give up. Harsh, critical comments are the hardest thing for me about the writing life, and the enemy knows it. As a mom, hard hearts and disobedience make me want to give up. I find myself wondering if these boys will *ever* change. But I've learned the secret to overcoming when I want to give up...

Fight anyway.

When a mama is having her moment—when she's done, deflated, depressed, and ready to denounce motherhood altogether—she needs to know that she can keep fighting, and that there's a very specific reason why a mama can keep fighting for her children, even when every ounce of her fight is gone.

A mom can fight for her children because God is fighting for her.

> And Moses said to the people, "Fear not, stand firm, and see the salvation of the LORD, which he will work for you today. For the Egyptians whom you see today, you shall never see again. The LORD will fight for you, and you have only to be silent" (Exodus 14:13-14).

Do you remember what it felt like to have your mom or dad cup your face in their hands and tell you they believed in you? Or maybe a good friend just looked you in the eyes one day and said, "I've got your back." It's kind of like that, only much better, because this time, the person who's on your side, fighting for you in ways you can't even understand, is God Almighty—the one who loved you so much he let his Son suffer and die in your place.

- When you're convinced that thing you just did is going to be the thing your daughter talks about with her therapist later in life, he's fighting for you, giving you strength to go ask for forgiveness.

- When you can't imagine going back in that house, back to the noise, back to the bickering, back to the same thing every single day, he's fighting for you, giving you energy to open the door.

- When that loved one sucker-punches you with words meant to crucify, not edify, he's fighting for you, making his Word and his heart available to help you choose the truth.

- When you're scared and vulnerable, he's fighting for you, protecting you within his will.

God is on your side. He loves you. You're the apple of his eye. He's got your back. So you keep fighting, mama, because the God of the universe is fighting for you.

Pray with me?

Lord, today, I need to believe you're fighting for me. The hardest part of the Christian life is being able to believe what we can't see. But then, that's what faith really is, right? Help me have faith enough to get through the fight—to fight for my family, not against them. In Jesus's name, amen.

Going Deeper

- What circumstances make you want to give up?
- How does it make you feel to know God is fighting for you?
- Do you believe it?

A mom can fight for her children
because God is fighting for her.

He Is Gentle

*Take my yoke upon you, and learn from
me, for I am gentle and lowly in heart, and
you will find rest for your souls.*

MATTHEW 11:29

Stacey

I sometimes think I would like to start a Martha fan club. Poor thing, she gets all the criticism and sweet devoted Mary gets all the praise. Martha is like the fashion *don't* of the Bible. I can picture her in my mind standing in her modest kitchen, hands in the bread dough, stirring a pot or two of something wonderful, and trying to get the serving platters off the shelf all at the same time. She was trying so hard to serve her master. Trying oh so hard.

Honestly, I think she meant well. I think she had the strength of responsibility that turned on her in these types of moments. She could not just sit and let the Savior of the world go without a decent dinner. She had to be the one to do it of course because Mary was nowhere to be found. *Typical.* I think she was stirring that pot and muttering under her breath the words of a martyr. *"Well, I guess I'll have to serve the meal as well, since I'm the only one around here who is actually working to feed all these people."*

She might have just had about enough of all the work falling onto her capable shoulders when she mentioned to Jesus that Mary was not really doing anything to help her out in the kitchen. I think he looked at her mussed-up hair and stressed-out expression and saw straight into her heart. He spoke her name twice. I think Jesus said it with more grace than we can imagine.

> Oh Martha, Martha, you are so anxious and concerned about a million details, but really, only one thing matters. Mary has chosen that one thing, and I won't take it away from her (Luke 10:41-42 THE VOICE).

My heart just breaks for Martha. I get her. I am her most days distracted by a million little and not-so-little details. I want to serve my family and love them like Jesus—I really do. But, I confess I'm anxious at times by it all.

But Jesus turns to me just like he did to Martha that day and he calls me by name. He probably has to say it more than twice because we have four girls in our house and they are always talking. He knows this, of course. With all grace and gentleness he looks at me and speaks the words of Matthew 11:29 over my heart:

Stacey. Stacey. Stop with all the doing. Come away with me. Learn my gentle ways. Find rest for your weary soul.

Of course he knows that finding the rest I need doesn't come naturally to me. I need practice. What he really is offering me is a sweet pause from all my activity in the midst of my crazy busy life. The psalmist calls this pause *Selah*. Selah is simply the place at his feet where I can gaze into his gentle eyes and find deep soul rest.

Every time Jesus comes to me he comes gently. He can't come

any other way. Gentleness is not his personality or a characteristic he portrays. *Gentle is who Christ is.* So even when he wants to do business in my life or he brings power or a word of conviction, he does it gently.

I really wish we could have seen Martha's response to Jesus's gentle invitation to take a seat with Mary. I'm not sure what she did, but I know in those moments when I hear him calling my name once, twice, or four times I must respond. Today, I'm going to leave the dishes in the sink and let the floor be dirty for a few minutes so I can grab a cup of coffee and sit in my big red chair to learn a little more of his gentle loving ways. Would you like to join me? There is a place right next to me. I promise.

Pray with me?

> Gentle Lord, I am anxious today for all the undone things on my list. What I need more than anything is a Selah moment to sit with you and receive the rest my weary soul needs. I'm so grateful I can find that at your feet today. In Jesus's name, amen.

Going Deeper

- When are you most like Martha?
- How do you learn his gentle ways on a daily basis?

Gentle is who Christ is. So even when he wants to do business in my life or he brings power or a word of conviction, he does it gently.

He Sings Over You

The LORD your God is in your midst, a mighty
one who will save; he will rejoice over you
with gladness; he will quiet you by his love; he
will exult over you with loud singing.

ZEPHANIAH 3:17

Stacey

I make myself a cup of coffee and sit down in my big red chair. It is not even six in the morning. In the last week I have slept a sum total of ten hours. I am severely lacking and beginning to think sleep is a thorn in my flesh and I will never make friends with it as long as I am this side of heaven. I'm coping, but barely.

I caught a glimpse of myself in the mirror as I walked by. A messy bun and dark circles have become my wardrobe. I don't feel pretty anymore. I am wearing my weariness for all to see. I feel and look a shell of the girl I used to be. To top it off, yesterday I yelled at my girls. Like a lot. I was the yeller mommy who could not yell loud enough to get them to do what I wanted them to do. I don't feel pretty and I have not acted pretty.

I sit down, put my feet up on the ottoman, and wrap my hands around the warm mug. I show up here almost every morning because I am broken and in need of the truth of God to wash over me fresh. He meets me regardless of what I look like or how I've been behaving. I close my eyes and release my heart to his. His response to me is a song. My God is quite the crooner.

> Is that a joyous choir I hear? No, it is the Lord himself exulting over you in happy song (Zephaniah 3:17 TLB).

The Lord himself sings over me. He bursts into song over you as well. Disney and their happy little working songs have nothing on the Lord Jehovah. In the middle of our lives, mussed-up hair, dark circles, and craziness, the existing supreme God is singing over us. I know this because in this passage, the people God is singing over have not been role model followers. They have rebelled. They have lived in oppressive exile. They are scattered and lost. But guess what? God doesn't sing over them because they are great. He sings over them because he is great and he loves them with a powerful transforming type of love.

Matthew Henry says, "The great God not only loves his saints, but he loves to love them." His song woos them back to himself and into the relationship he longs to keep with them. He longs to restore them and shelter them from their enemies and oppressors. He loves to love them like this. It is who he is and always has been.

Do you remember records? I mean actual size 45" put them on the record player and play them type of records? You bought it for the A side song, but each record had a B side as well—a bonus song by the same artist. Do you know God's song has a B side as well?

The bonus of his joy-filled, wooing, happy song is peace. His song will calm your fears and hold you in peace. It has that type of power. Isn't that a beautiful truth to grab on to today?

Oh, but wait! There is one more thing you need to know. His song comes with an invitation to join him. He loves to hear you singing as well. "Sing aloud, O daughter of Zion; shout, O Israel! Rejoice and exult with all your heart, O daughter of Jerusalem!" (Zephaniah 3:14). Your mighty savior God wants you to sing too. I know you may not feel like singing, but I promise when you join him, your heart will change. I do this loudly and unashamed some days. Usually, the song we sing together is "Swing Low, Sweet Chariot." I'm not sure why this is the song we sing on the hardest days, but it works. My girls think I'm nuts. But, really I'm singing a duet with the Lord.

I know today might be one of those days for you. Like me, you don't feel very precious. You may feel a little used and wondering how you are going to survive the next twelve hours until the kids go to bed again. I wonder if you could just close your eyes and listen with your heart to the tender and sweet song God is singing over you. As he is rescuing, protecting, and gathering you to his side today, he is ever bursting into a joyful song because you are his daughter. Receive it and let it soften your heart today. Let it dig down into the depths of your weary soul and breathe life and peace into your day. That is what it is meant to do.

Pray with me?

> Lord, let me hear the song you sing over me today as
> I pack lunches, listen to constant chatter, referee arguments, and cook dinner. Let it revive my heart and draw
> me closer to you. In Jesus's name, amen.

Going Deeper

- What song can you hear God singing over you? What is the one truth he is repeating over and over again?

- Can you join him in the song by faith?

Close your eyes and listen with your heart to the tender and sweet song God is singing over you. As he is rescuing, protecting, and gathering you to his side today, he is ever bursting into a joyful song because you are his daughter.

He Hears You

*Because He bends down to listen, I will
pray as long as I have breath!*
PSALM 116:2 NLT

Brooke

George Muller was a man convinced of the power of prayer. In the 1800s, Muller answered a simple call from God to make his name known. By opening an orphan house, Muller determined to show the world that God could and would provide for our every need. He ran the orphan house not by monthly supporters, not by speaking at local churches to ask for money, and not from any government grants. He ran the house through prayer, simply asking God to provide for their every need.

And God did.

George Muller's simple, childlike faith challenges me to believe that God will come when I call. We live in a noisy, busy world. Before I wrote this chapter, I prayed and asked God to help me shut out everything else that might distract me. Why? Because there is *so* much to distract me! Dings here, messages there, a never-ending to-do list, laundry on the couch, children calling "Mommy!"...and the list goes on and on. Sometimes, the noise of life makes me forget I serve a God who bends down to listen. I forget he's there, waiting for me to call on him for help, and I go about my day totally missing out on the power of a relationship with him.

Psalm 116:2 has become something of a life verse for me. An encouragement, if you will, to keep praying—keep communicating—with God. Not necessarily because I want him to do something, or even because I need to share my heart with him. I pray because I know God bends down to listen.

The God of heaven, who created me, you, and everything around us, bends down to listen to the hearts of those he loves and cherishes the most. That does something in my heart. Knowing that God is not far away, looking down from heaven, surprised by my need. He's here, right now, waiting for me to talk to him. He's the God of our moments because he wants to be in our moments. Not an afterthought, but every thought.

George Muller says this in his autobiography:

> The primary business I must attend to every day is to fellowship with the Lord. The first concern is not how much I might serve the Lord, but how my inner man might be nourished. I may share the truth with the unconverted; I may try to encourage believers; I may relieve the distressed; or I may, in other ways, seek to behave as a child of God; yet, not being happy in the Lord, and not being nourished and strengthened in my inner man day by day, may result in this work being done in a wrong spirit.*

---

* George Muller, *The Autobiography of George Muller* (New Kensington, PA: Whitaker House, 1984), 138-39.

Friends, if we don't nourish our souls by talking to the Lord, asking him to be with us in the moments of our day, we'll never have the fullness of life the way he desires us to. We'll go about our business, struggling through the challenges we face, and wonder why God doesn't feel near.

Maybe it's because we didn't ask him for help?

Here are three things to remember as you're learning to call on the God who hears you:

1. God doesn't have to *come* to your aid. When you're a believer, he's already there (Deuteronomy 31:8), just waiting for you to tell him you need him. There's nowhere you can go that he can't see you or can't hear you, and he's the God who bends down to listen, inclining his holy ears to your cries for help.

2. Train yourself to call on him. A few years ago, I decided to start "praying on the hours." My prayer life wasn't as rich as I wanted it to be, and I desired to feel closer to the Lord throughout my day instead of just first thing in the morning. So I prayed when my alarm clock went off in the morning, thanking the Lord for rest and asking him to be with me in the next hour. Then, I set the alarm on my phone for the next hour. When it went off, I thanked him for being with me in the previous hour and asked him to go before me into the next.

I did this for a solid week before it became a habit. But the process changed the way I interact with God on a daily basis. Try it and see if it doesn't make you more aware of his presence with you. Your prayers don't have to be formal or long. Sometimes I was driving when the alarm went off. But I committed to praying every hour, no matter where I was, and if my boys were with me I prayed out loud whenever possible to help them understand how much we need Jesus to be in our day. It was a great learning experience!

3. Choose to believe he hears you even when you don't feel like he does. When we lost our third baby to miscarriage I felt like my prayers were hitting the ceiling, and I wondered if God was near. I didn't *feel* like he heard me, didn't *feel* like he was close by. But I was able to keep going because I know my feelings don't define what's true—the Bible does. Weariness, fear, hopelessness, hurt...those are all feelings. Hope is a choice.

A choice to believe that what God's Word says is true, *is* true.

I may not *feel* like God hears me, but the Bible says he does. So if what I feel and what the Bible says is true don't line up, guess which one needs to change? Me.

Maybe you?

Pray with me?

> Lord, I'm bombarded by *all. the. things.* the very moment I get out of bed. Children who want to be fed, beeps and buzzes from my phone, a house that has already self-destructed. Somewhere in there, my heart longs to find a way to give you the most sacred of my space. Help me find a way. Come be the God of my moments, not as an afterthought, but every thought. In Jesus's name, amen.

Going Deeper

- It doesn't really matter how many things are vying for our attention during the day. Kids crying, to-do lists, business, or ministry—if we don't take advantage of the continuous fellowship God offers us, we're missing out, and probably not functioning to the fullest of our ability. Ask God to give you eyes to see how important this is to your well-being and to that of your family, and then give

it the attention it deserves. Choose hope over your feelings and watch God meet you in your moments.

• What are some practical ways you can invite God into
  your moments?

∞∞∞

He's the God of our moments because he wants to be in
our moments. Not an afterthought, but every thought.

∞∞∞

His Word Is Alive

*For the word of God is living and active, sharper
than any two-edged sword, piercing to the division
of soul and of spirit, of joints and of marrow, and
discerning the thoughts and intentions of the heart.*

HEBREWS 4:12

Brooke

When I was a young Christian I knew I should be reading the Bible. I believed it was the truth and that I should be obeying what it had to say. I embraced that mindset early on, by the grace of God, but I didn't know how to activate it, or actually make it make a difference in my life. There was a disconnect somewhere between what I read and how it affected my heart.

Notice I didn't say how it affected my *actions*. It did affect the choices I made while I was growing up, but mainly out of fear. I didn't want to do the wrong thing and then have to explain it to my parents. I was a "good girl" in school, and most of the choices I made to walk in obedience to God's commands came from a place of wanting to appear like I had it all together, not because there was a love relationship between me and God.

I grew up thinking the Bible was a list of things to do or not to do, not a tool to deepen and strengthen my relationship with Christ. Certainly not a book that held the power to change my life.

But now I know the Bible is unlike any other book out there. It's not just a book of good stories about men and women who gave their lives to an important cause. Those books are valuable (I read them to my boys every day in school) and help us aspire to be a better person, but they're not like the Bible.

The Bible is alive.

The words we read on the pages of our Bibles are living, active, and the very breath of God. The Bible is actually "activated" even if we don't choose to embrace its benefits in our lives, because the words have the power to change us from the inside out, "piercing to the division of soul and of spirit, of joints and of marrow, and discerning the thoughts and intentions of the heart" (Hebrews 4:12).

What does that mean?

God gets you. He knows you. He understands you, and the words of Scripture come directly from him.

Knowing this, we can go to God's Word with expectation—expecting to hear from him, expecting the words on the page to transform our hearts. But so many Christians still struggle to feel anything when they read God's Word. It just doesn't seem true to them because they don't experience anything when they read it—especially in the hard times of life.

Before we jump into the hows of activating the Word of God in your life, I want to say this: What you feel and what is true may be two different things. Just because I sometimes feel abandoned by God doesn't mean I am. His Word tells me he will never leave me nor forsake me (Hebrews 13:5), so when I find myself feeling abandoned, I have to choose to believe I'm not. Most of the time, when I make that choice, my feelings will soon follow the choice of my heart.

I've found that there are five main ways to activate the word of God in our lives. Some of them are simple and you can start doing them right way. Others may take some time and a commitment to opening your heart up to God in a new way.

1. Open it. When my oldest son first started playing the fiddle, he wasn't very good. He was pretty terrible the next day too, and even a few weeks after his first lesson. He learned to play "Twinkle, Twinkle Little Star" quickly, but little violins have terrible sound quality, so he still sounded pretty bad.

Now, almost five years later, he's performed "Ode to Joy" in front of 500 people with his little brother and is gearing up to compete in a local fiddler's convention over the summer.

Get in the habit of spending daily time in your Bible, even if it's just to read a psalm and a proverb. It may not come easily, but just as my son needed time spent practicing his instrument to improve, we need time in the Word of God to begin trusting it.

2. Know it. As you spend more and more time reading your Bible you'll see something amazing start to happen! You'll find yourself thinking about or living in a certain situation when a verse you just read (that applies to what you're going through) will pop in your head! That's God. That's the Word being alive and active in you, and it's amazing!

I can't count the number of times I've been comforted by a verse at just the right time. Whether God drops it in my heart or the heart of a friend, he chooses to use his Word to comfort, correct, sustain, and build us right when we need it most.

But if we don't open it and don't know it, that won't happen.

3. Speak it. When I was younger I battled fear. One of the ways

I went to war against this attack of the enemy was to speak God's Word out loud, and even though God has given me a significant measure of healing in this area, I still speak Bible verses out loud when I'm afraid.

My favorites are Psalm 4:8 and Psalm 23:4. "In peace I will both lie down and sleep; for you alone, O Lord, make me dwell in safety." This one gets spoken when I'm trying to fall asleep. "Even though I walk through the valley of the shadow of death, I will fear no evil, for you are with me; your rod and your staff, they comfort me." I say this one when I'm walking into a dark house alone and feel threatened. Sometimes, I even just say Jesus's name out loud, because it's the name above all names (Philippians 2:9-11) and is mighty to save (Zephaniah 3:17).

Speaking a verse or two out loud—whether you're afraid, or confused, or hurt—reminds us of what's true, and has the power to make peace settle in our hearts.

4. Use it. If you come to my house, you'll see sticky notes all over. Written on them are Bible verses that focus my attention on Jesus and help me remember what's true. I have them strategically placed in the house where I need them most. For example, there's one in the bathroom to remind me that my greatest need is Jesus. Why? Because the bathroom is where I tend to go when I want to lock myself away.

I also have my favorite scriptures printed out and framed around our house. I use them as reminders and as prayers. When I walk by my sons' door, I pray Psalm 92:4 because it's hanging in a frame outside their room. These are simple, inexpensive ways to fill our hearts with the Word of God. I can't necessarily afford those beautiful framed scriptures from my local Christian bookstore, but I can afford a five-dollar frame from Wal-Mart and a little ink from my printer.

5. Love it. This one may be the most important of all, because loving God's Word starts with loving him. If we don't have a deep sense of gratitude and love for God, we won't love his Word.

How do we "fall in love" with God? For me, it's a simple matter of remembering all he sacrificed for me while I was still stuck in sin (Romans 5:8). I'm so grateful for forgiveness from my sin, so grateful that I'm not who I was, so grateful to have right standing before the Lord, so grateful that I can call on him, so grateful that he sees me and loves me, so grateful that he protects me and provides for me...so grateful that all I can do is love him in return.

Because of that, I want to know him, know his character and his ways, to the best of my ability. I love the Bible because it's how I get to know him better and learn about his great love for me.

The Bible has amazing power to transform our lives when we open it, know it, speak it, use it, and love it. Why wait?

Pray with me?

> Lord, I've been walking for too long without the power of your Word in my life. Today, and every single day of the rest of my life, I'd like to see its power. Right now, I commit (to the best of my ability) to open it, know it, speak it, use it, and love it. Help me have the strength to do it. In Jesus's name, amen.

Going Deeper

- What's one practical step you can take right now, starting today, that will activate the Word of God in your life?

- Make a commitment to get started. Then, make a list of other things you can do that will serve as your goal for the next several months. Put them on a sticky note where you'll see them often and ask God to give you the faith to walk them out.

∞∞∞∞∞∞∞∞∞∞∞∞∞∞∞∞∞∞∞∞∞∞∞∞∞∞∞∞

We can go to God's Word with expectation—
expecting to hear from him, expecting the words
on the page to transform our hearts.

∞∞∞∞∞∞∞∞∞∞∞∞∞∞∞∞∞∞∞∞∞∞∞∞∞∞∞∞

He Is Able

*If you throw us into the blazing furnace, then the God
we serve is able to rescue us from a furnace of blazing
fire and release us from your power, Your Majesty.*
DANIEL 3:17 THE VOICE

Stacey

I learned my Bible stories at a young age. My mom was a Sunday school teacher for 25 years and she taught me all the stories through singing a tune. I can call her any time and ask her to remind me how one of the songs goes, and she will quickly belt it out for me.

I realize now, all these years later, how many foundational truths are packed in these stories. Faith, hope, and the love of God flow through each and every one. One of my all-time favorites had a line like this: "God was there he never let them go—Shadrach, Meshach, Abednego."

Do you know this story? Three young Hebrew men were given a choice to bow down to an idol made by man or take a one-way ticket to a furnace of fire. They chose to honor Jehovah God by refusing to bow to the fake one. This greatly angered the king (who, by the way, looked a lot like that idol), and he was about to make good on his promise.

But Shadrach, Meshach, and Abednego had eyes of faith that saw beyond the temporal and through to the eternal. Their response, with respect, implied they knew two things:

1. God was able to save them physically.
2. God would certainly save them spiritually.

Although I think they had a hunch, Shadrach, Meshach, and Abednego were not sure if God would save their physical bodies. But they had no doubts he was *able* to do so. They knew for certain that if he chose not to, he would carry their spiritual bodies to a better place. The story heats up seven times hotter and the three are thrown into the furnace on the orders of the outraged monarch. The fire was so hot the guards who tossed them into the flames were killed instantly.

When the king looked into the furnace he saw not three figures, but four. Because "God was there he never let them go." The observers were dumbfounded:

> The officers, prefects, governors, and king's advisors moved closer to see *what had happened to* these men. *They, too, could hardly believe their eyes.* The fire had done nothing to harm these men. Their hair was not singed. Their clothes were not scorched. They didn't have the faintest smell of smoke on them (Daniel 3:27 THE VOICE).

They were unharmed. Not one hair singed. Not even the hint of smoke on them. Because when the flames burned the fiercest, God did not let them go. He stood with them.

I know some days as a weary mom you feel like you are in the midst of a fiery furnace. No one is obeying, the house is a mess, and you are faced with going to the grocery store with all the kids in tow. Can it get any hotter in here? Are you fanning yourself too? I want to remind you that in the middle of that swirling hot mess of a day, God will never let you go. He is with you in the mess. We know he is able deliver you from it by sending a free babysitter and a house cleaning service because he is God. He is able to do that. Most of the time he chooses to stand with us in the midst of it all. I think he does this because he knows the fire is a place to refine us and make us like him. He also knows other people, namely our kids and friends, are watching to see how we get through it. Maybe they will look at us dumbfounded too.

How did you survive today?

How is your heart so calm?

Are you actually *smiling*?

"Yes. God stood with me. He is my strength. He never leaves me in the flames of a messy day alone," you will say, pointing to him. We know he is able to deliver you *from*. But wouldn't it be even more of a testimony to deliver you *through*?

Pray with me?

> Lord, you never let me go, no matter the swirling mess around me. You are using these days to refine me and make me more like you. Today I look to you. You are able to deliver me from the hard days, but choose often, instead, to deliver me through it. Be glorified in my life. In Jesus's name, amen.

Going Deeper

- What does a hot mess of a day look like for you?

- How do you know God is standing with you in it? Can you point to him as the reason for your hope today?

◇◇

The fire is a place to refine us and make us like him.

◇◇

His Word Is True

Truly, truly, I say to you, you will weep and lament, but the world will rejoice. You will be sorrowful, but your sorrow will turn into joy.

JOHN 16:20

Stacey

Some days we need a friend to look us in the eyes and tell it like it is. My friend Lisa is a truth teller in every good way. Right after my first daughter was born I asked her if I was ever going to feel rested again. She looked at me and said, "No. Not like you did when you were younger and you could sleep all day if you wanted to. Your tiredness will shift and not be as severe as it is with a newborn. But you are a mom now. You will be constantly laying down your life and pouring out every ounce of energy you have. So there will always be a degree of tiredness in your life from now on."

This was a truth I desperately needed to hear. I was chasing sleep like a dog chases cars, hoping eventually if I ran fast enough I could win the game. Hearing this truth gave me the freedom to keep my expectations realistic and settle into my new life as mom. I also was more grateful when I did catch a quick nap and not fuss that it wasn't two hours long.

Jesus is the ultimate truth teller. He said of himself, "I am the way, the truth, and the life" (John 14:6). Today he speaks truth to us through the pages of his Word. We need to come back to this truth every day, because left to our own devices we will naturally gravitate toward lies. These lies will keep us buried in discouragement and despair. They will cause us to swim in mommy guilt and keep us from fulfilling our God-given role as mom. A daily dose of truth will transform us. It also gives us his perspective to see things as he does. In fact, it has the power to set us free (John 8:32).

I love that Jesus was constantly saying, "Truly I say to you" and then telling his followers an absolute truth. The word *truly* actually means "amen." When put at the beginning of a sentence, the speaker is saying "You can absolutely believe this is true." In John 16:20 you will notice Jesus said it twice. It was almost like he was taking them by the shoulders and looking into their eyes and saying: "Please believe me completely when I say this: You will have great sorrow and the world will rejoice. I'm not kidding. But trust me, your sorrow will be turned to joy."

What was Jesus trying to tell them? He was preparing them for the days ahead when he would die on the cross. His disciples would be devastated while the enemies of God rejoiced. This would not last forever: the disciples' sorrow would be transformed to joy. Why? Christ was going to conquer death for them and pay the penalty for their sins. He was going to give them a joy that would last forever.

This truth matters to us as well. Jesus conquered death and because of this we can trust his Word to be true. Nothing we face today is impossible for him. He wants to tell our hearts what we need to hear most. You and I need a fresh encounter with it every day. And then we need to speak it over our hearts in the minutes and hours that make up the rest of that day. We need to tell it to our children. They need to see us believing and clinging to it because this will impact their lives as well.

When you put the word "amen" at the end of a sentence it means "may it be fulfilled." When we all agree with one accord we are basically saying, "Lord, let the truth of your Word be fulfilled in me."

So, sweet friend, can I get an amen?

Pray with me?

> Lord, your truth can and will transform my life. I want to know it and hide it in my heart so I can tell my children as well. May it be fulfilled in my life and theirs. In Jesus's name, amen.

Going Deeper

- What lie have you believed lately?
- What truth from God's Word can you speak over your heart to remind you he can be trusted?

Nothing you face today is impossible for Jesus.

He's the God of Miracles

Does he who supplies the Spirit to you and works
miracles among you do so by works of the law, or
by hearing with faith—just as Abraham believed
God, and it was counted to him as righteousness.

GALATIANS 3:5

Brooke

Merriam-Webster defines a miracle as an extremely outstanding or unusual event, thing, or accomplishment. I think they're wrong.

More often than not, God works in the small, not-so-grand events in our lives and calls that the miracle.

If you read *Hope for the Weary Mom*, you're familiar with the story of how God healed my heart after the miscarriage of our third baby. It's not like my miscarriage was uncommon. According to the American Pregnancy Association, somewhere between 10 and 25 percent of women in childbearing years will have one. That's one in four on the high end, meaning that in a room full of 100 women—perhaps at my next Bible study at church—25 of us could've had one. That's a lot of miscarriages, a lot of broken dreams, a lot of hurting hearts.

I had wanted the miracle to be that my baby's heart would be beating, but it wasn't. God had other plans for that tiny life and didn't give me the desire of my heart. No, the miracle in our situation wasn't big, flashy, or obviously divinely given. It required eyes to see the small things around us, something I might not have had had the miracle I really wanted been mine.

We took a family vacation in the fall of that year. One week together, away from the everyday, waiting for my body to miscarry our third baby. I sat in the sand with the waves lapping my toes and watched my husband play and romp with my boys like I was seeing them for the first time. I watched arms and legs flapping and flopping in the water, heard little voices screaming, "Watch *this*, Mommy!" and held the hand of my man strong, knowing that God was giving me a gift, even as he took another gift away.

That week at the beach, as I grieved the loss of our baby, I found something I had lost.

Hope.

It was in my husband's hand as he held mine, assuring me of his presence.

It was in the laughter of my children as they played with reckless abandon.

It was in the wind, blowing our hair straight up and everywhere.

It was in the waves, reminding me of the strength of God's voice.

It was in a smile, a giggle, a touch. I saw my children display humility, perseverance, forgiveness, and grace. I watched my husband take out the trash, sweep, empty the dishwasher, and give me time to get lost in a few good books. I saw the good and overlooked the bad for the first time in a long time.

And I realized I'd spent so much time on my knees about the

things that were wrong that I'd forgotten to look at the things that were right.

It's easy to get stuck in the mess, isn't it? We fall so far down in the pit that it's hard to see the blue sky at the top anymore. Gloom and doom become the norm. We yell more because we see fault more, and we forget to look at the positive in our lives.

Can I challenge us, friends? What if today we committed to looking for the good in our families? It's there, I promise. You may have to dig long, hard, and deep to find it. You may have to pray and ask God to reveal it in areas you thought were beyond his gaze, but it's there somewhere, waiting to give you hope.

The miracle God gave me at the beach that day was small, and might seem insignificant to some, but it truly changed my entire outlook, making healing possible in a situation that felt cruel and hard.

And isn't that the way God works most of the time? In the small?

We think that to qualify as a miracle, something has to be huge and bright and clear to all who see it—outstanding, unusual. Two little boys playing in the sand with their daddy is pretty common. There's nothing all that unique or unusual about it. But for me, it was as if God was pouring light into my hurting soul. I looked at their faces, their bodies, their smiles. I heard their giggles, their gasps for air, their squeals of delight. And I knew. This was the miracle. Life had passed, but life had come. Life was still there waiting to be lived, waiting for me to reach out and grab it.

Sure, sometimes God does something big, and we know it was him and he gets the glory. But the greatest miracle of all is fully embracing the everyday gifts God gives. Are we giving him the glory in those too?

When your toddler smiles at you.

When your teenager calls home.

When your husband remembers...

When God provides for that small need and seems to say, "I see you."

When the sun shines through the trees just so...

When the mama deer walks in front of you with her two speckled babies following close behind.

When the evening temperature is cool enough that you want to scoot a little closer.

When there's laughter instead of fighting.

When the breeze lifts your hair and blows it away from your face.

These, along with one million other tiny things, are the miracles that matter—the things we should remember to praise God for and allow to bring a smile to our faces.

But I'm afraid we're too busy for these kinds of miracles. Life is fast and it takes work to slow it down. And most of us? Well, we don't do the work it takes to hear the "still, small voice" of God (1 Kings 19:12).

But what if we did?

What if, starting today, we asked the Lord to open our eyes? What if we truly meant it when we said, "Slow me down, Lord, so I can see you in the small things"? What if instead of saying, "Go! Go! Go!" we said, "Stop! Stop! Stop! This moment will never happen again. Let me breathe it in!"

I know it's hard to go slow, and I know there are days when it's next to impossible not to rush. Practices need to be attended, dinners need to be fixed, project deadlines must be met. But if I hadn't been sitting on my parents' front porch this afternoon thinking about what I wanted to write in this chapter, sipping some ice water, and relaxing on my grandparents' old bench, I would've missed that mama deer and small bird hopping in the grass in front of me.

The wind chimes would've chimed with no one to hear; the breeze would've blown without touching my hair.

And I would've missed the small.

Let's not do that ever again.

Pray with me?

> Lord, I want to see the small miracles you bring my way every day. Would you open my eyes to them today so I can really see all the things I have to be thankful for? Help me slow down so I can truly see. In Jesus's name, amen.

Going Deeper

- When was the last time you stopped and soaked in the goodness of God in your everyday life?

- If it's been a while, take a leap of faith, put down whatever you're working on, and go do it right now. Ask the Lord to meet you there, and trust him for a miracle.

◇◇

God works in the small, not-so-grand events in our
lives and calls that the miracle.

◇◇

He Has Plans for You

*For I know the plans I have for you. Plans
to give you a future and a hope.*

JEREMIAH 29:11

Stacey

My plan was always to be a mom. I think it is really the only thing I knew for sure I wanted to be when I grew up. I'm grateful my plan of being a mom lined up with God's plan for me. He blessed us with our first daughter fifteen years ago and three more since. Each time my eyes first saw them, I was amazed God allowed me to be their mom. What I didn't know then was that there would be many days to follow when I would wonder why he chose me for this role. I have had my fair share of days when I felt inadequate. I'm a broken mess of a mom. I don't have all the answers. My children have needs far greater than I can meet. What on earth was God thinking?

Perhaps he was thinking, "I have a good plan for Stacey. My good plan is for her to be a mom to these four girls. This plan is going to give her a future where she will need to depend on me moment by moment. This plan will lead her to cling to hope like she never has before. My plan will help make her into the woman I want her to be."

I see that now, even on days when my life feels aimless and I fail more times than not. I believe he is working out his purpose in my life through my motherhood. I also have come to understand two other things:

First, God chose me to be the mother of my children because they would need me.

Second, God gave me the four children I have because he knew I would need them.

The person God made me is perfectly suited for my girls. I'm the best mom for them. I am especially the best mom for them as I lean deep into the Word of God and draw upon his strength for long days. They need me to need him as I walk alongside them. I am the mom he wants to disciple them. I am the mom who their hearts bend toward. He has made it so.

But what I'm realizing lately is God's plan goes both ways. Each one of my girls has been used by the Lord to uniquely draw out of me a strength to hone and a weakness to develop. They are like magnifying glasses in my life. He uses them daily to show me the work he wants to do in and through me. They not only need me to be *their mom*. I need them to be *my daughters*. They are part of his plan in my life as he himself parents me.

This has never been clearer in my life since the birth of my fourth daughter. My husband really wanted us to have a fourth child. We weren't, contrary to popular opinion, trying to have a boy. He simply felt in his heart our family was not complete. I prayed. God led me to a place of peace with adding to our family as well. You know what? Both my husband and God were right. Of course our family was not complete without our youngest. She has been a sweet gift I didn't know I needed. Ironically, she looks the most like me. She is a mini-me to the core.

She was part of God's plan. Since then, I have seen my deep need of God's grace. I think before she came along I was pretty much mothering in my own strength. God knew what it would take to lead me to a place of complete dependence. It isn't her personally, but the overwhelming task of raising these four girls together that brings me to a place of needing God like never before. He knew this is what it would take. He has also used this vulnerable place to call me out from hiding behind my veil of *fine*.

And this plan? God says it is good. It has a purpose. It will lead to a future. Some days, I don't see it. But when I look back on my mothering journey I see his handprint all over it. As I look ahead, we have big milestones in front of us—driving and graduations to name just two. I know his promise to be true. There is hope on every page.

Pray with me?

> Lord, your plan was for me to be the mother of my children. You use them every day to show me my need of you. You say this plan is good and I'm going to follow you every step of the way. In Jesus's name, amen.

Going Deeper

- How has God changed you through mothering?
- Why are you the mother for *your* children?
- What is it about your children that God uses to make you more like him?

∞∞∞∞∞∞∞∞∞∞∞∞∞∞∞∞∞∞∞∞∞∞∞∞∞∞∞∞∞∞

This plan? God says it is good.
It has a purpose.
It will lead to a future.

∞∞∞∞∞∞∞∞∞∞∞∞∞∞∞∞∞∞∞∞∞∞∞∞∞∞∞∞∞∞

He's the Lover of Your Soul

The LORD opens the eyes of the blind. The LORD lifts up those who are bowed down; the LORD loves the righteous.

PSALM 146:8

Stacey

 turn the light off and let the nightlight clipped to her bed fill the room with patterns of dancing stars. We sit in the rocking chair my husband bought for my first Mother's Day and begin the back-and-forth motion I've used to rock her and her three sisters to sleep. We settle in with her blanket and she asks me, "Mommy, sing 'Jesus'?" I know exactly what she means and I start the familiar refrain:

"Jesus loves me this I know, for the Bible tells me so..."

She says "Again!" over and over and so go the next twenty minutes. When I lay her down I tiptoe out of the room and gently shut the door. I get to the stairs and I wonder why it is so hard to let that be the song of my heart as well.

Do you struggle to believe it too? I think we all do. But the truth is God makes it his mission to flat-out love us. He not only tells us over and over again he loves us; he demonstrates that love. He frees us from sin, nourishes our hearts, and cherishes us as his beloved children. He daily wants to open our eyes to the love he has for us.

Bob Goff says in his best selling book *Love Does*, "That's because love is never stationary. In the end, love doesn't just keep thinking about it or keep planning for it. Simply put: love does."* So what does love do?

Love lifts the burden when we are bowed low: Once there was a woman who was bent low under the burden of life. Luke tells us "She had been bent double for eighteen years and was unable to stand up straight." Jesus saw her and called her to himself while he was teaching in the Synagogue. She could not raise her eyes to meet his, but his love met her anyway and he said, "'Dear woman, you are healed of your sickness!' Then he touched her, and instantly she could stand straight. How she praised God!" (Luke 13:12-13 NLT).

Love opens our eyes when we are blind to it: On a different occasion a blind man named Bartimaeus heard Jesus was coming his way so he shouted with all of his might for "Mercy!" The crowds told him to be quiet, but Jesus said, "What do you want me to do for you?"

"My Rabbi," the blind man said, "I want to see!'"

And Jesus said to him, "Go, for your faith has healed you." Instantly the man could see, and he followed Jesus down the road (Mark 10:51-52 NLT).

Love keeps moving in my life too. Especially on days when my weary eyes are too tired to see it and I'm bent down underneath the table picking fish-shaped crackers off the floor. Just like I grab my daughter and pull her up to my lap and sing over and over to her

---

* Bob Goff, *Love Does* (Nashville, TN: Thomas Nelson, 2012), xvi.

while moving back and forth, his love keeps rocking my heart with the constant refrain, "Yes, Jesus loves me. The Bible tells me so." Because you see, love tells and love does. I can open his Word every day and read thousands of verses that tell me how much he loves loving me. I can also see with my own eyes the love he stretches in front of me in the beauty of a sunrise on the beach or the warmth in the hugs from girls while I'm making their lunch.

God's love is the ultimate show and tell. And now it is time for me to believe it.

Pray with me?

> Lord, your love does amazing things. You lift my burdens and open my eyes. Thank you for loving to love me so passionately. I receive and believe that today. In Jesus's name, amen.

Going Deeper

How has God shown you lately he loves you? What expression of his love means the most to you as a mom?

∞∞

Jesus loves me, this I know, for the Bible tells me so.

∞∞

He Is the Treasure Within You

But this beautiful treasure is contained in us—
cracked pots made of earth and clay—so that the
transcendent character of this power will be clearly
seen as coming from God and not from us.

2 CORINTHIANS 4:7 THE VOICE

Stacey

I lived veiled for years. I hid the broken places of my life because I was under the impression I needed to have it together to be used by God. If he was going to ask me to raise my girls and lead other women, surely I needed to hide behind *fine*. Who would really want to know about my daily struggle with weariness, anyhow? I thought I was the only one. I thought others would see my weakness and run from me, glad they were in a much better place.

I was wrong and wrapped in a lie that defeated me daily. I saw brokenness. God saw a chance to shine his light through my life. I saw ugly. He saw a treasure peeking through. I saw weakness. He saw a place his strength could be perfected. I saw women running away from my struggles. He saw a white flag going up and women running toward me carrying their own. He was right.

I'm not sure why God chooses to place his greatest treasure in everyday clay vessels. I imagine him walking up and down the department store aisles and choosing the everyday household pieces over finely crafted china detailed with artisan gold inlay. He purposely dwells within us, knowing we are common and prone to chipping here and there. He knows why. My part is to trust.

And where has my weak and frail earthen vessel cracked lately? Sleep has been far from me, so I am short on patience and long on complaints. I feel tired and tried by every situation. My girls must be on to it because, let's face it, I'm not hiding it well. They are pushing me and the cracks just keep getting bigger. There is a part of me that wishes my cracks would lessen with age, but it seems to me the longer I walk with this treasure of the gospel inside me, the greater the crevices become. And Jesus smiles and says, "Exactly."

So less of me just equals more of him. His light shines through the gaping holes in my life and not only does he shine forth—you get to look in. See, it works both ways. Remember when I was putting on the veil everyday? I was simply hiding the treasure within me by trying to appear stronger than I was. I had it all wrong. Matthew Henry said, "The weaker the vessels are the stronger his power may appear, that the treasure itself may be valued the more."*

There is truly a hope-treasure within this weary mom. I don't have any tips, tricks, or tools to share with you about motherhood. What I do have is the dynamic power of God living inside me, able to strengthen me for the calling of motherhood he has placed on my life. He has made me a storehouse for his treasure. Have mercy! Can you believe this girl who needs four cups of coffee every sunrise gets

---

* Matthew Henry, *Matthew Henry Commentary on the Whole Bible (Complete)*, "2 Corinthians 4:7", http://www.blueletterbible.org/Comm/mhc/2Cr/2Cr_004.cfm?a=1082007.

to inhabit that truth every day? Oh, the truth is even better than we can imagine. Because what is true for me is also true for you.

My friend Emily said, "What amazes me about Jesus is that he doesn't remove the cracks entirely. Sometimes he smooths them over and mends bits and pieces, but he always leaves some sort of evidence—some way for his presence to be filtered through the pain that caused them in the first place!" His grace is found in the fact that I am mended and cracked at the same time.

Hindsight is a beautiful thing. I can look back over the past few years and remember e-mails, tears, and encouragements from other moms who really thought they were the only ones who felt weary. "How did you know? Did you read my journal?" they would declare. I knew because I was waking up every day feeling cracked and broken. But God saw my brokenness as an opportunity, not a defect.

Finally, I'm beginning to as well. I'm pretty sure the only thing that is going to make a difference in me today is the truth from this verse. This earthen vessel has the treasure of Jesus within it. His power can overcome my cracks. His light can shine forth. I can take joy in knowing my brokenness only magnifies the hope that is within me.

Pray with me?

Today, may my weakness bring you more glory because you shine brighter in my broken places. Let these mended cracks be what draws others into my story and closer to you. In Jesus's name, amen.

Going Deeper

How has motherhood broken you and where do you see the chance to let the light of God's power shine through? Can we do that by faith together today?

This earthen vessel has the treasure of Jesus within it.
His power can overcome your cracks.
His light can shine forth.

He Speaks to You

When he has brought out all his own, he goes before them, and the sheep follow him, for they know his voice.

JOHN 10:4

Brooke

My husband has a saying that makes everyone laugh. He'll say something funny (or annoying, as the case may be) and I'll respond with a heavy sigh. You know the kind, right? That deep intake of breath and the forceful exhale that follows? I'm sure you've done it to your husband or kids too. But when I do it, my husband turns to me and says, "Did you just 'heavy sigh' me?"

It's funny because he somehow manages to use a descriptive phrase one might find in a play script ("the actor turns away from the scene with a heavy sigh...") as an action verb. Now, after years of usage and two small boys who constantly have me rolling my eyes and "heavy sighing," it's become a normal part of our McGlothlin Home for Boys vocabulary.

So the other day, as I had an incredibly big decision to make, I found myself in the midst of the "heavy sigh." In fact, I think my entire conversation with God was one big heavy sigh. I desperately wanted to hear his voice, but I was having trouble discerning what was him and what wasn't.

In many ways, God seemed silent on the issue. I prayed, and searched Scripture, and talked to trusted friends I knew would point me to him, but still, no clear answer came.

You could say that God was just refusing to speak to me during that time, and I'll admit it was a bit frustrating. What I really wanted was to wake up to a big neon sign hanging over my bed the next morning that said, "Do this!" And while that might have scared my husband half to death, I would've embraced it, so ready was I to do exactly what the Lord required.

Obviously, that didn't happen. But it did get me thinking a bit about the way God speaks to his children, and how we can know he's spoken to us when he does.

I've never heard the audible voice of God, but I do know when he speaks to me. In a meaningful sheep/shepherd analogy, John 10:4 confirms that because we (the sheep) belong to God (the shepherd), we know his voice. It doesn't say we might know his voice. It says his sheep *know* his voice. In other words, it's done. It's not something we have to grow into; it's there—this deep knowing that says, "that's my Savior speaking to me."

In biblical times, shepherding was a fierce, difficult, and often life-threatening job. Scriptures tell us David killed a bear while shepherding his flock, not something I've ever done as a writer, for sure. In order to get those sheep, known for being stubborn, to follow him, the shepherd would've been through hell and back. So by the time they'd been together for a while, those sheep would've known the voice of their master. He was the one they'd follow given another option, because he represented safety, protection, and comfort.

As I've walked with the Lord over the years I've come to this conclusion: God won't always speak to me about everything I bring to him. Sometimes, I just have to base my decisions on what I already know to be true.

I've spent a lot of time in the Word since I became a Christian. And while I certainly don't know everything about the Bible, I do have a deep relationship with the words written in it because I've spent time pouring over them, memorizing them, loving them, and speaking them over my life. God's words written in the Bible are his life and breath to me. I'm not just saying that to sound hoity-toity, either. The fact is that God's word *is* our life and breath. Without it, we're living a sub-par experience of life, less than what he intends for us.

I've also, by the grace of God, learned how to apply the Word *to* my life. Because God has sent mentors and role models my way, I've learned how not to just read the Bible, but put it to use in my life. I'm living it—slipping, and picking myself back up daily—but living it.

These things combined are powerfully important. Lysa TerKeurst, in her book *The Best Yes,* says this: "When we've done what we need to do to acquire the knowledge and insight of truth, then the discernment of that truth is there. We must learn to trust and use that discernment."[*]

Exactly.

When I'm making a decision and God seems to be silent on which direction I should take, I often lean on what I already know about his character to help me move forward. I can move forward to a confident future because God has spoken truth to me in the past. I *know* him, therefore I can follow him without needing a neon sign.

---

[*] Lysa TerKeurst, *The Best Yes* (Nashville, TN: Thomas Nelson, 2014), 37.

We've been to hell and back together. He's my place of safety, protection, and comfort, and he's never let me down. I have no reason to believe he ever will.

I also find confidence in my decisions by keeping a focused eye on what God is doing around me. Henry Blackaby, in his now famous study called *Experiencing God*, challenges believers to look around to see what God is already doing in their lives and join him in it. For this particular decision, I was asking the Lord to show me whether or not I should go somewhere to speak. In order to get there, I needed to front some money of my own, so I prayed for three weeks asking the Lord to provide the money, thereby showing me he wanted me to go.

He didn't.

In fact, during that three-week time period, our dishwasher broke, our dryer broke, and our lawn mower broke. Every extra dime we might've had went to fixing those fairly necessary appliances. I had to take care of my family before I could go take care of someone else's family, and because of that, the answer was clear. There was no biblical reason I could think of to prevent me from speaking at this conference—it's a solid, Christian conference that I've been to before and loved—but a good look at my family's circumstances, or what was happening around me, provided me with all the direction I needed. If that hadn't been enough, the visible lifting of stress from my husband's shoulders when I told him I wasn't going sealed the deal. My family needed me at home. So I said no.

And I felt great doing it.

I knew, beyond a shadow of a doubt, the answer to my decision was "stay home," but it was the process of trusting what I already knew about God that led me there, not the neon sign I had hoped for. Honestly, it was better to come to my answer this way because it taught me to trust God's influence in my life.

As believers, those Jesus calls his own, we've been given the ability to hear his voice. Whether he gives us clear direction or not doesn't really matter—he still speaks. If we're listening in the right ways—reading, praying, acting on his Word—we'll hear.

Pray with me?

> Lord, I confess, sometimes I'm too busy to hear your voice and I just don't know the way to go. As I intentionally spend more time in your Word, would you plant it in my heart so that when I truly need it, it's there helping me to see the way? In Jesus's name, amen.

Going Deeper

- Have you ever doubted that God speaks to his children? If you've experienced a season of quiet, you probably have. Take a moment to look back at that time in your life with fresh eyes and evaluate it through the lens of what you just learned.

- What was God speaking to you through your knowledge of him, prayer, and your circumstances?

<hr>

I can move forward to a confident future because God has spoken truth to me in the past.

<hr>

He's Holding You Together

He is before all things, and in him
all things hold together.
Colossians 1:17

Stacey

I have a great love for the beach. One of my favorite things to do is watch the sun make its first appearance over the water. On the perfect beach morning last year, I woke up before dawn. I grabbed my cardigan, brewed a cup of mediocre coffee, and slipped out onto the porch doing my best not to wake the sleeping babes on the pullout sofa. The view was about eleven stories high, which made it pretty much perfect. I sat myself in a folding chair, put my feet up on the railing, and waited.

The first light was gentle and engaging. It said, "Wait patiently; there is more to come." The birds dove down to grab a breakfast treat from the water. A man placed his fishing pole firmly in the ground and put his hands in his pockets. He was waiting too.

Suddenly, without warning, the light multiplied and the water was dancing with pinks and yellows. I was watching the most beautiful love story unfold. The sun was lifting over the ocean vast and deep and it moved my heart along with the waves crashing on the shore. I can't explain it, but in this moment I was held by the greatness of God. I tasted my coffee and took it all in. This was heavenly. My heart was full. I felt small and it was good.

Sometimes my smallness is a gift. Other times my smallness feels useless. Life looms and I can't keep up. I am like Alice shrinking in Wonderland, trying to figure out the magic potion to drink to make myself bigger than the next problem or task ahead. It is in these moments I have a choice to make: Will I see my smallness as a gift or a curse? Will I let it drive me to Jesus or will I let it drive me crazy?

Jesus. Go ahead and speak his name aloud. He is the one who existed before each and every thing in this world was created. When God spoke, Jesus was the Word and the witness. He is the one who, by his dynamic power, is holding all of those same things together. Ray Stedman writes, "When Paul uses the phrase, 'all things by him hold together,' he is speaking of our Lord's power to sustain and to prevent breakdown."* Guess what that also includes? It includes you and me. He keeps us from falling apart, literally.

We can be overwhelmed by the truth of who Jesus is instead of being overwhelmed by life. We can be held together knowing he is able. He is unshakable. He can handle whatever our day brings. When I place my smallness in his capable hold-it-all-together hands I am wrapped in his glorious greatness and peace washes over me. This is easy to do when I have a glorious sunrise dazzling before my eyes. But what about when I have to take my girls to Target and they instantly turn into small crazy people? When every look from a passerby is one of judgment? It is in these times I need to be reminded

---

* Ray Stedman, "Master of the Universe," sermon, http://raystedman.org/new-testament/colossians/master-of-the-universe, accessed July 30, 2014.

that God is working on my behalf and Jesus is holding me together. He can dazzle in awesome splendor in those moments too. I assure you his holding me together in Target is as much of a miracle as making the sun appear each morning. He sustains me. He is the reason I don't break down and fall into the ugly cry by the time I reach the checkout. He holds weary moms together from the inside out. This verse can be a sweet reminder for us all. Are you singing a hallelujah chorus over this truth today? I know I am. Trust me, the folks at Target are too.

Pray with me?

> The mere fact that you are holding me together, Lord, is a gift. I don't have to keep it together because that is your job. This is so freeing. Let me be overwhelmed by you and nothing else today. In Jesus's name, amen.

Going Deeper

- What part of God's creation helps you feel small in a good way?
- When you feel simply small and overwhelmed, how can you remind your heart that he is holding you together from the inside out?

God is working on your behalf and Jesus is holding you together.

He Never Changes

Jesus Christ is the same yesterday and today and forever.
HEBREWS 13:8

Stacey

I have lost the ability to sleep past 6:30. It is true that my addiction to coffee may have a slight connection to this, but I also blame my heritage. My grandma woke up around 5:30 every day so I feel like I may be winning slightly in that department.

Every morning when I wake up and make my way to the same kitchen, the darkness of the morning is a friend to me because it hides the usual left-in-the-sink dishes. Slowly the sun comes up and I see spread before me a day much like the one before—one where I'm already starting from behind. It rarely changes. Most days unfold like the one before. Monday slides into Wednesday with not so much of a change in pace and I just keep getting up, drinking coffee, and playing my part as wife and mom.

True, on some days I crave a little more excitement than spilled milk dripping through the cracks of my kitchen table. But

113

monotonous doesn't have to be equated with *boring* or *meaningless.* The monotony I dread means security, consistency, and a foundation for loving my family well. Think about it with me for a minute.

- Where I see monotony, my children see my presence.
- Where I fear getting lost in laundry, my girls see acts of service.
- When I feel like I'm nothing special, I get to be the one who runs to them when they cry out during the night. I get to be a superhero in their eyes.

I know it may be hard to believe, but I see this in my own life when I think of Jesus. His sameness is a promise to me. The truth of his consistent presence in my life is one of the greatest gifts he has given me. When the world screams by at the speed of flashy status updates and Twitter tells me one more time the news is filled with dread, my Jesus stands unchanging and all grace in my life. There are days I am able to take one more breath and rest in his hope because I can count on him to be "the same yesterday and today and forever."

- Sameness is dependable.
- Sameness is comfort.
- Sameness is strong.

When it is wrapped in the flesh of Jesus I actually consider sameness to be a treasure. Another word for this is *immutability.* Jesus is unchanging in our ever-changing world. He is the same yesterday, today, and forever. He is always himself. Every day in every way we can trust the fact that Jesus is going to show up and be himself in our lives. He is power and love and discipline in my life. He is savior, friend, and the one who goes before me. He is willing to walk beside me. He is my hope for today because his name was hope in the very beginning of time.

The writer of Hebrews also tells us that when God needed to swear a promise to Abraham he swore by himself, because he alone is true and unchanging. As the Voice translation of the Bible puts it, "That hope is real and true, an anchor to steady our *restless* souls" (Hebrews 6:19).

The sameness of Jesus is an anchor for our restless souls. I want my girls to see me clinging to that anchor. I don't want them to have a mom who is disillusioned by a monotonous life, but grateful to have a front-row seat to the little everyday parts of life that can either be blessings or burdens. I'm praying I will allow Jesus to be *the same* in me and they will see that with eyes blazing over breakfast on Monday mornings.

Pray with me?

> Lord, your sameness is indeed my treasure. I pray I will let my children see the consistent pursuit of who you are in my life day after day. May they be blessed with a mother whose true hope rests in the anchor of who you are. In Jesus's name, amen.

Going Deeper

- What part of your sameness is a blessing to your kids today?

- How does it feel to know that tomorrow, when you wake up, Jesus is going to be just as real and loving as he is today?

◇◇◇◇◇◇◇◇◇◇◇◇◇◇◇◇◇◇◇◇◇◇◇◇◇◇◇◇◇◇◇◇◇◇

Jesus is my hope for today because his name was hope
in the very beginning of time.

◇◇◇◇◇◇◇◇◇◇◇◇◇◇◇◇◇◇◇◇◇◇◇◇◇◇◇◇◇◇◇◇◇◇

He Prays for You

*I do not ask for these only, but also for those
who will believe in me through their word.*

JOHN 17:20

Brooke

made a commitment of faith when I was just nine years old.
Wide-eyed and trembling in the cold baptismal waters, I
nodded my head in agreement as the pastor of my small Baptist
church asked me if I had decided to give my heart to Jesus. After it
was over, my mama and a group of sweet church ladies whisked me
away to a Sunday School room to dry me off, get me warm, and
make me presentable. I sat in the pew for the rest of the sermon
with wet hair and a warm heart, knowing I'd just done something
very important...something that would shape the course of the rest
of my life.

The truth is, I don't remember one single day when I wasn't
aware of God on some level. From the tender age of nine onward
(and maybe even before), I've known God had a plan for my life,

believed he was good, and sensed him watching over me. But in spite of those things—baptism, belief, knowing—I didn't walk closely with him until I was almost 21 years old.

For twelve years I wore the title of Christian well, but if you'd looked inside my heart you wouldn't have seen much to prove it. I like to call myself a Pharisee, because truly that's what I was. Jesus describes this state of the heart when he's talking to the religious leaders in Matthew 23:25: "Woe to you, scribes and Pharisees, hypocrites! For you clean the outside of the cup and the plate, but inside they are full of greed and self-indulgence."

It's painful to think about, but plain to see that this verse described the way I was living—trying to make my own way while keeping God at arm's length. Knowing that his rules and regulations were meant to protect me, but choosing to believe my feelings—what I could see, taste, touch, and hear—over the truth of his Word.

It was a recipe for disaster, and one that left me completely vulnerable before the God I had surrendered to as a young girl...and needed to surrender to again.

But as it turns out, my self-built disaster was the best thing that ever happened to me.

I sat on my bed in my college apartment surrounded by reminders of my own attempts to build a kingdom that glorified Brooke, and I wondered how I would find my way back. Ironically (or maybe not so much), I had decided to take a New Testament class that semester, and I remembered that I needed to do some reading in the book of John for homework. I picked up my class Bible, turned to John chapter 17, and began to read about the final hours of Jesus's life here on earth.

In verses nine through sixteen, Jesus prayed for his disciples. He knew the struggles they would go through after his death and resurrection, and as his own life hung in the balance, he took the time to cover them in prayer, asking his Father to protect them and lead them well. But verse 20 is different. Look at it closely with me: "I do not ask for these only, but also for those who will believe in me through their word."

Friend, do you realize who Jesus is talking about in that verse? It's you. It's me. It's every single person who has ever believed the story of the life, death, and resurrection of Jesus. That's a lot of people...and Jesus took the time to pray for us before e died.

As I read those words, and the true meaning of them became clear, a new feeling washed over me that drowned out the feelings of despair and hopelessness I had experienced just a few moments before.

Jesus prayed for me.

Me. Within a few hours of that prayer he faced one of the most gruesome deaths ever recorded—a death meant for me, a punishment for my sins—and instead of worrying about himself he prayed for me.

For you.

Isn't that the real meaning of the cross? That God's love for us was so great, his devotion to us so sincere, that he would send his one and only Son to die on the cross and take the punishment for our sins? He's all about love—a love so great that it's concerned with the object of its desire (you and me) even in the face of great pain and trial, humiliation, wrongful accusation, and death.

Today, let that kind of love wash over you like it did for me that day in my apartment, now so many years ago. In your darkest days, the ones where you're tempted to despair and wonder if God truly hears you, truly sees you, remember that he prayed for you, and according to Scripture, still does (Hebrews 7:25).

Pray with me?

Lord, I'm not sure I really understand how you could have had me on your mind when you were enduring the cross. But you did. Help me to grasp the fullness of that gift today. I want to know the fullness of your love so that I can love others more fully. In Jesus's name, amen.

Going Deeper

- Do you have a story about how God met you in your mess? A story that shows the depth of his love for you? Tell someone about it today!

- If you never have, get some time alone today and talk to Jesus like he's sitting right beside you. Pour out your heart to him knowing that as you do so, he's going to the Father on your behalf.

◇◇◇◇◇◇◇◇◇◇◇◇◇◇◇◇◇◇◇◇◇◇◇◇◇◇◇◇◇◇

In your darkest days, the ones where you're tempted to despair and wonder if God truly hears you, remember that he prayed for you.

◇◇◇◇◇◇◇◇◇◇◇◇◇◇◇◇◇◇◇◇◇◇◇◇◇◇◇◇◇◇

He's Your Rescuer

*Therefore, say to the people of Israel: "I am the Lord. I
will free you from your oppression and will rescue
you from your slavery in Egypt. I will redeem you
with a powerful arm and great acts of judgment."*
EXODUS 6:5-7 NLT

Stacey

I imagine there were days when Israel cried out for rescue from
the deserts of Egyptian slavery. There must have been times
they strained their eyes from looking at the horizon, wondering
when the rescue was coming. There might also have been days when
they forgot the promise and simply went about the backbreaking
work without hope.

But God never forgot. From his perspective, he was not late in
keeping his promise. He was coming with power and great acts of
judgment. He had a plan, and not for one minute did he ever consider doing anything different.

My friend Robin needed a rescue one day. She was walking home
from class our senior year at Indiana University during the blizzard

of the century. The odds were not in her favor as she set out uphill in the biting, windblown snow toward the apartment we called home.

She did not know, and I could not tell her in the days before cell phones existed, I was making my way toward her. I had left work early and knew Robin would be getting out of class soon. I knew the way she took and decided I would drive it back to our apartment to pick her up. She was overwhelmed by the storm; all the while I was on a rescue mission. She had no idea rescue was coming, and that was the best part of my plan.

I made my way slowly down the one-way streets in my little red car, straining my eyes to find her. Where was she in this sea of white? Had she taken the bus instead?

Finally in the distance I saw her heavily bundled-up shape trudging slowly through the rapidly falling snow. I was so excited to find her, I started blaring my horn. I honked furiously.

Meanwhile, Robin was cold, wet, tired, and possibly a bit cranky. She heard a noise behind her that sounded like an obnoxious driver. I was still some distance away and she had no idea it was me. She grew more annoyed by the moment, thinking to herself, "Doesn't the driver know I'm doing the best I can? I can't get over any further! There is no sidewalk to walk on. I can't do any better than this!"

When she finally had enough of my honking, she turned completely around (she had five layers on and couldn't just turn her head) and saw me. The look on her face was priceless. It changed instantly from annoyance to one of overwhelming joy. She was rescued and she knew it. Even after twenty years, I still remember that day vividly.

Rescue is sweet.

There are many days as a mother I remember to cry out for my rescuer to come to me and bring me hope. I remind him of the thousands of times he has promised to never leave me. There are just as many days I am buried under the efforts of making lunches, doing laundry, and loading the dishwasher and I don't. I am like a slave in Israel who has forgotten he always keeps his promises and rescue is coming. Overwhelmed and working in my own strength I cry out, "I'm doing the best I can."

See, just like my friend Robin could not see her rescue from my perspective, I can't see from his. He is making his way toward me—all within his perfect timing. He is coming with his eyes deadlocked on me the whole time. When my eyes meet his, overwhelming relief and joy flows.

He is our rescue.

He always has been.

He always will be.

Even when our weary eyes don't see it coming.

Pray with me?

> Jesus, you are always on time when I need you most. When my best falls short, you breathe grace over my weary days. You rescue me. You pursue me. I'm grateful for your promises and I'm clinging to them today. In Jesus's name, amen.

Going Deeper

- When do you most need a rescue?

- Do you believe that God's promise of rescue is for you as well?

God is making his way toward you—
all within his perfect timing.

He Redeems You

*Who redeems your life from the pit, who
crowns you with steadfast love and mercy.*

PSALM 103:4

Brooke

$\mathcal{I}$f you'd looked at my life from the outside when I was in my
twenties, you wouldn't have seen anything to indicate I was living in a pit. I came from a secure, loving family, had everything I
needed growing up, had a car to drive and a place to live, and was
attending college and preparing for graduate school.

Pretty good, right?

You might've looked at me and thought, "Certainly she has nothing to complain about. Everything in her life is going right."

You might've thought that, but you would've been wrong.

In today's Pinterest-perfect world, it's hard to see others beyond
what they portray online...*really* see them I mean. Oh, it's easy to see
what they do, or what they wear, or how incredible their children's

birthday parties are...ahem...but to really see *them*? I don't think they want us to.

The Internet makes it easy to present the image we *want* others to believe about us rather than what truly is. But even before the Internet was a big thing, I still looked good on the outside while I was crumbling on the inside. I needed rescue, but no one knew.

Sometimes, it's easy to see those around us who are in need of redemption and rescue. Other times, they're harder to spot.

As I've worked with the Seed Company some over the last few years, I've realized that God is moving in big ways all over the world. The Seed Company is a Bible translation ministry, and their work is incredible. They see the hand of God moving and restoring in some of the worst situations you could imagine.

One day, after a call with them, I remember crying out to the Lord and saying, "Why can't you move like that here, Lord? I'm thrilled that you're redeeming and protecting these precious people, giving them your Word for the first time in their own heart language, but I want to see you do miracles like you're doing there, here. Why aren't you?"

The answer, I think, is because we're less needy, less desperate here in the United States. Or at least we think we are. We have nice homes, cars to take us from one place to another, gyms to work out in so our bodies don't deteriorate too quickly, and churches on every street corner. People in other countries live in shacks, eat from trash dumps, walk barefoot, and work out their bodies by sheer manual labor. And churches? Well, in some places they'd get beheaded for even speaking that word out loud.

They thirst for a word from God, anything at all, while we drown in convenience and excess. Maybe God can move more freely there, picking people up out of an obvious and sometimes literal pit because they actually know their need. We don't know our need because we have everything we need.

At least that's how it was for me.

But there's a need that goes much deeper than the physical. It may be easy to see "the pit" people are living in all across the country, but there's a pit in our hearts, too. We just can't see it because, for the most part, we all think we're okay. The fact of the matter is we're not okay. Not at all. We may have conveniences and luxuries 90 percent of the world has never known, but in many ways they're better off than we are.

We're the epitome of Matthew 15:8, which says, "This people honors me with their lips, but their heart is far from me."

Fifteen years ago I would've told you God had been good to me and that I was grateful for his gifts. But what I really meant was that I was thankful to not be poor, to have nice clothes, and to have money to spend for the things I needed. I'm not sure being thankful for my salvation would've crossed my mind. In fact, I had no idea how completely overtaken by sin I really was.

Sin doesn't have to be this huge thing, like murder or adultery. Sin can be jealousy, lust, gossip, caring more about ourselves than we do others, or anything, really, that causes us to choose something or someone else over God.

When you define "the pit" that way, it's clear to see that we're pretty bad off. We drive around in our shiny new cars, thanking God for providing for everything we need, but our hearts are far from him, not realizing that he cares more about what's in our hearts than what's under our rears.

Your life has been in the pit. It might not be a pit you have to dig through just to find food, but it's a pit nonetheless. And if you're a believer—if you've put your faith and trust in Jesus to save you from your sin—you're redeemed from it. Jesus bought you, shed the same innocent blood for you as he did our brother in Rwanda who hides his family under a bed to escape the militant army killing people just outside. Your need and mine is just as great. It's just harder to see.

How desperately we all need Jesus, even—and maybe especially—when it doesn't look like it on the outside.

Pray with me?

> I forget so easily, Lord, how desperately I need you. Help me to never take my salvation and your work in my life for granted. Help me remember how desperate I am for your guidance and love in my life, and today, work a miracle through me. In Jesus's name, amen.

Going Deeper

- I used to get very sad when I thought about my past sin. I have so many choices I wish I had made differently. Shame and regret would fill my heart and cause me to want to run away. But now that I understand the depth of what Christ saved me from—even though it might not look like much to those watching from the outside—I let those memories turn my heart to Jesus in gratitude and worship. I'm not sure we can ever experience the depth of gratitude Jesus deserves until we rightly understand the depth of our sin—visible or not. Take a moment to reflect on your past sin. Let the reality of it sink in, saying, "Yes, I did that. I'm guilty." But don't stay there.

- As you begin to see yourself in a more correct light (a sinner in need of salvation), allow the truth of what

Jesus did for you to take the place of any shame you might feel. *This* is what redemption is. Jesus paid it all; all to him we owe. Sin had left a crimson stain all over our hearts and bodies; he washed it white as snow.

∞∞∞∞∞∞∞∞∞∞∞∞∞∞∞∞∞∞∞∞∞∞∞∞∞∞∞∞∞∞∞

Your life has been in the pit. It might not be a pit you have to dig through just to find food, but it's a pit nonetheless. And Jesus has redeemed you from it.

∞∞∞∞∞∞∞∞∞∞∞∞∞∞∞∞∞∞∞∞∞∞∞∞∞∞∞∞∞∞∞

He Is Your Refuge

He who dwells in the shelter of the Most High will abide
in the shadow of the Almighty. I will say to the Lord,
"My refuge and my fortress, my God, in whom I trust."
Psalm 91:1-2

Stacey

When my third daughter was a newborn, my husband gently let me know that he was going to start traveling a few times each year internationally for work. Soon after, he left on his first trip that lasted about fifteen days. At the time I had three children under the age of six. A friend of mine sent me a free babysitter and a pizza because she was worried about me. Bless her heart, I was worried about me, too.

I come from a long line of women who worry well. You might say we are certified dreamers of all the bad stuff that can and probably will happen. I knew I was going to have to find a way to get over my genetic predisposition to worry—and fast! I would need to act like the thirty-five-year-old I was, learn to trust God, and not fear things that go bump in the night. And trust me, when you are alone in the house with children there are lots of things that go bump in the night. They are also quick to call out for "Mommy!" when they do.

So I prayed. I asked God to give me something I could cling to that was greater than my fear. I didn't want my husband to worry about me and miss the opportunity he had to be part of the work he was being asked to do. I remember reading once about Ruth Bell Graham, the wife of the Reverend Billy Graham. She said Billy's job was to go and her job was to stay. His job was to preach to the nations. Her job was to be home when he was finished. I wanted this to be true of me too. About this same time my friend handed me a prayer book packed with prayers and Scripture to pray in all situations. It was on the pages of this little book shared between two moms that I fell in love with Psalm 91 and the sixteen verses contained within it.

I studied it. I read it over and over again. And every night when I lay down in my bed with my babies nearby, I spoke it aloud over my home and heart. Pretty soon, the fear of what could happen was replaced with what was happening:

- I was sitting in the presence of the Lord.
- His presence was covering me like a shadow. I was protected.
- My trust was growing.
- I was able to find him a precious refuge for my lonely nights.
- He was my protector and defender.

- I could go to sleep easily because he was awake at night watching over me.
- I had nothing to fear morning, noon, or night.
- He was ordering his angels to guard us.
- No evil would come close to my door.
- I could call on his name and immediately he would rescue me.

Head knowledge is a beautiful thing, but what I needed was to live this out in front of my girls. The psalmist said I needed to abide in the shadow of the Almighty. Do you know where the shadow is? As close to God as I could get. I needed to seek him, and as Charles Spurgeon calls it, be his "constant guest." So even with my husband gone across the ocean and needy children wanting to be fed, cleaned, and taken to school, I continued to seek quiet time with him. I started my mornings early in the pages of his Word and I spoke Psalm 91 to him before I went to bed. I told him, "You are my refuge and my shield." I claimed it. Suddenly I was the child running to her father in heaven and he was wrapping his big daddy arms around me telling me he was my safe place. I had nothing to fear. For the first time, I believed him.

Eight years and probably twenty trips overseas later, I still whisper Psalm 91 as I drift off to sleep. The funny thing now is, I don't say it because I am scared. I say it because I remember I don't have to be.

Pray with me?

> Lord, cover me with your wings; be a strong refuge for me especially when fears run amuck in my heart. I believe you to be my fortress and my protector. I will trust in you. In Jesus's name, amen.

Going Deeper

Are you alone for any reason at this time in your life? Can I ask you to make Psalm 91 a nightly prayer as you claim God as your refuge?

<hr />

Abide in the shadow of the Almighty. Do you know where the shadow is? As close to God as you can get.

<hr />

He Is Your Hope

*May the God of hope fill you with all joy and
peace in believing, so that by the power of
the Holy Spirit you may abound in hope.*

ROMANS 15:13

Stacey

Last spring I bought my girls a new box of sidewalk chalk. They love to spend hours creating masterpieces on our driveway and I enjoy seeing their sweet pictures underneath my feet as I'm climbing into my minivan. Sometimes I even join them and add my own doodles and creations. One day, while I was in the middle of writing *Hope for the Weary Mom*, I scrawled the word *hope* on the concrete and drew rainbow concentric circles all around it. It was surrounded by cupcakes, stick figures, and cat drawings made by my girls. Hope had been on my mind and I was wrestling it once again in my heart.

And then it poured rain for hours. We watched the chalk drawings fade into the gutter and went to bed with the pitter-patter of rain in our ears. The next morning we walked outside to go to church and my daughter said, "Mom, look! How come your hope drawing didn't wash away?" There in the middle of the still-damp slab of concrete, as strong as the moment I drew it, was the word *hope*. I said, "Well, honey, you can't wash hope away, I suppose." I smiled. I knew the lesson was for me.

I had been studying a passage from Romans about that same time. Tucked inside it is a prayer Paul prays for fellow believers. It is one of the best reminders of why we can't wash hope away. First of all, God himself is our source of hope. He is hope. The original language in this verse tells us he is the author and foundation of hope. Hope is not a personality trait God has, like you and I are friendly or not on some days. Hope is at the core of who he is. Every time he moves in your life it is with hope.

Emily Dickinson wrote, "Hope is the thing with feathers." This phrase has always confused me. I'm pretty sure it means that hope flies when nothing else does. For some reason this always makes me feel a little melancholy instead of infused with strength. But Romans 15:13 is a verse that makes me want to stand on the chair and say, "Yes and amen." My hope is a real person. Not a bird that flies to and from. And my source of hope never leaves me.

The other thing I have learned from this amazing little prayer of Paul is the power for hope to overflow in my life is from the Holy Spirit. Another way to think of it is as a believer in Christ, the power for your hope to abound already lives in your heart through the person of the Holy Spirit. The Greek word for power here happens to be one of my favorites. It is *dynamis* and means "inherent power." Think of a stick of dynamite—it has all the power within it to explode. The Holy Spirit within you has all the power you need to explode with hope. Our part is believing he has all the power. Our belief in him stirs the hope within us.

Life is going to have its fair share of rain. Sometimes the rain will come with a case of the drearies and make you want to curl up in a ball on the sofa with a good chick flick. Other times the rain will bring a storm of epic proportion. The wind will howl, the house will shake, and your heart will wonder how much more it can take.

But hope will not wash away. This is your promise. Your source of hope will never stop seeking to pour it fresh into your heart. You don't have to wish for hope. You already have it. He is your hope.

It reminds me a little bit of Dorothy and her bejeweled slippers. She went through a storm too. The answer she was looking for was right underneath her feet.

You have the power for hope to abound in your life. It is from the author of hope who lives in your heart. And no storm will ever wash it away.

Pray with me?

> Lord, may your abounding hope ignite in my heart as I
> put my faith in you. Let joy and peace be the evidence
> of this truth at work in my life. In Jesus's name, amen.

Going Deeper

Is a storm in your life making you feel hopeless? Take this prayer of Paul and pray it daily over your life: *May the God of hope fill you with all joy and peace in believing, so that by the power of the Holy Spirit you may abound in hope.*

⬦⬦⬦⬦⬦⬦⬦⬦⬦⬦⬦⬦⬦⬦⬦⬦⬦⬦⬦⬦⬦⬦⬦⬦⬦⬦⬦⬦⬦⬦

Hope will not wash away. This is your promise. Your
source of hope will never stop seeking to pour it fresh
into your heart.

⬦⬦⬦⬦⬦⬦⬦⬦⬦⬦⬦⬦⬦⬦⬦⬦⬦⬦⬦⬦⬦⬦⬦⬦⬦⬦⬦⬦⬦⬦

He Forgets Your Sins

As far as the east is from the west, so far does
he remove our transgressions from us.

PSALM 103:12

Brooke

You know those skeletons in your closet you hope no one ever finds out about? I have a few of those. I think most everyone does. Mistakes we made in college, stupid choices made in haste, financial decisions with long-term effects, shortcuts that ended up hurting more than helping.

Choices truly do have the power to cripple us, affecting our futures in ways we never thought they could. Sometimes they come back to haunt us and get thrown up in our faces when we least expect it. Even when we've repented for those sins and asked God to forgive us, we still remember, and that remembering can cause anxiety. But I've learned this: When forgiven sins resurface, it's never God who brought them up.

Every time the Lord brings me to a new season—a time of

excitement filled with new knowledge of him and new adventures with him—I remember. It happened the first time when I was getting ready to release my first book. One day I was happily putting together a marketing plan to help moms learn to pray for their sons, the next I was on my face before the Lord asking him to forgive me...again.

Like Moses, I asked God if he knew who he was dealing with. I told him I couldn't go where he was sending me, couldn't speak on his behalf. Why? "Because," I told myself, "they don't know who I truly am. If they knew about all my mistakes they wouldn't listen. I can't speak, Lord." I wanted to bury my head in the sand and make it all go away. I knew I was forgiven for my past sins, but there they were, coming at me again like fiery darts, making me want to run and hide.

Scripture tells us Moses told the Lord he wasn't eloquent enough for the mission he'd been given, but I've wondered if the real reason he felt inadequate was because of something else entirely. There's a small detail of Moses's life that doesn't get talked about all that much by biblical scholars, and yet there it is, in Exodus 2:11-12, buried in the sand.

> One day, when Moses had grown up, he went out to his people and looked on their burdens, and he saw an Egyptian beating a Hebrew, one of his people. He looked this way and that, and seeing no one, he struck down the Egyptian and hid him in the sand.

Moses was never publicly held accountable for murdering the Egyptian, but I'm sure he never forgot it. Could it have been part of the reason he felt unqualified for God's call on his life? We'll never know for sure, but I believe it was. Ironically, right after the murder, Moses did exactly what I felt like doing: He ran away.

In those moments before the Lord, when I felt like giving up, I wanted to run away. Several nights during that time I lay down in my bed to sleep only to be awoken by fear. Shame paralyzed me, and the only way I could work through the anxiety of it all was to pray under my breath, "I'm forgiven. I'm forgiven. I'm forgiven."

When the only way I could battle the fear was to wield the word of God, I began to suspect that I was dealing with an attack of the enemy. Scripture says the enemy of our souls comes only to "kill, steal, and destroy" (John 10:10), so the timing of this attack made perfect sense. I was getting ready to take a big step of obedience. I was already feeling vulnerable—because it's hard to put your heart and soul (in the form of a book) out on a platter for all the world to critique—and he was taking advantage of me by throwing reminders of all the things I'd ever done wrong right up in my face.

I wonder if that's how it was for Moses.

The enemy of Moses's soul, the one who desperately wanted God's great redemption plan to fail, wanted Moses to run away. He *wanted* the sins of Moses's past and the weaknesses of his present to affect all of our futures. So he attacked, leaving Moses feeling unworthy, unqualified, and unforgiven.

But God.

> But Moses said to God, "Who am I that I should go to Pharaoh and bring the children of Israel out of Egypt?"...God said to Moses, "I AM WHO I AM...say this to the people of Israel, 'I AM has sent me to you'" (Exodus 3:11,14).

You see, friend, it didn't really matter who Moses was or what he had done. What mattered was the identity and character of the God who sent him. Moses said, "Who am I?" and God replied, "It doesn't matter."

It doesn't matter.

Psalm 103:12 says, "as far as the east is from the west, so far does he remove our transgressions from us." When we're forgiven, we're forgiven.

All for God's glory.

Once we've repented of our sins, they're covered and paid for by Jesus's sacrifice on the cross. Done. Finished. When God looks at us he doesn't see all that might hinder us or all the ways our sins make us unworthy. He sees an opportunity for his name to be made great. He never brings up forgiven sins because they're not even on his radar anymore, and they don't affect what he's able to do through our surrendered lives! So if you're experiencing flashbacks of a life less godly, recognize it for what it is—an attack of the enemy—and deal with it accordingly. Remember that it doesn't matter who you are, only who God is.

Pray with me?

> Lord, sometimes I just can't get out from under the weight of my sin. It's like I'm bound up in a straight jacket and can't find the key. Today, help me to remember that your Word IS the key, the only key, and that you've given me the tools I need to overcome. I'm forgiven, I just need your help to remember it. In Jesus's name, amen.

Going Deeper

- Do sins from your past haunt you? Write each one of them on paper. Make a list of every sin you can think of that causes you shame.

- Now burn it. As you watch the list go up in flames, remember this verse and maybe even speak it out loud:

"As far as the east is from the west, so far does he remove our transgressions from us."

⟡⟡⟡⟡⟡⟡⟡⟡⟡⟡⟡⟡⟡⟡⟡⟡⟡⟡⟡⟡⟡⟡⟡⟡⟡⟡⟡⟡

When forgiven sins resurface,
it's never God who brought them up.

⟡⟡⟡⟡⟡⟡⟡⟡⟡⟡⟡⟡⟡⟡⟡⟡⟡⟡⟡⟡⟡⟡⟡⟡⟡⟡⟡⟡

He Pursues You

Therefore behold, I will allure her, and bring
her into the wilderness, and speak tenderly to
her. And there I will give her her vineyards and
make the Valley of Achor a door of hope.

HOSEA 2:14-15

Brooke

Lindsey saw him look her way and felt a mix of emotions hit her heart all at the same time—fear, excitement, attraction, and a hint of darkness—as their hands shook in greeting. Over lunch, she got to know him better and realized he was funny and charismatic. Her parched soul needed some rain, and when he sprinkled his charm her way the things in her that were dead started to wake up. Broken and desperately looking for sanctuary, she put her faith and trust in a man who in the same breath told her about Jesus and asked if she was still sleeping with her husband.

Over the next few months, as their conversations grew deeper and boundaries of appropriateness were crossed, he wooed her. And

despite the caution she felt in her heart, she let herself be wooed. So thirsty for healing from the wounds of her past was she that the wolf in sheep's clothing was hard to spot. To Lindsey, he felt like relief. His words offered her the first glimpse of God she'd ever really seen, even if encased in deceit. She thought, "Maybe this thing called God can help, and maybe this man who appears so full of God can get me to him."

Lindsey needed a friend, but in her desperate need, she made him her savior. In her words, "By the time it finally happened, we were both already lost. We continually compromised and justified our need, our selfish desire for far too long, flirting with disaster. I willingly betrayed my husband."

Time passed, and Lindsey hung in the balance between fantasy and crushing shame. At one point she dreamed of herself hanging over a foul pit. The only thing keeping her from falling was a giant hand gently holding her away from the flames.

Then, in an act she now sees as God's great mercy, they were found out, and the world turned upside-down. Stripped of everything, she sat across the table from her husband overcome with guilt and pain and heard him speak the words that God—the real God—would use to change her life.

"I love you; I always have. I will never leave you, and I am sorry I did not protect you from this."

True love removes our defenses and brings us to our knees. We're most like God when we show mercy.

It's God's kindness that leads us to repentance (Romans 2:1). Not his wrath, not eternal damnation, not happy platitudes that never penetrate the soul. Just the real, true, pure love of the Father. The book of Hosea, one of my favorites in the Old Testament, presents this amazingly beautiful picture of that kind of love as we watch God tell the prophet to marry a prostitute, have children with her, watch her go back to her old life—betraying him and their family—and then pursue her, offering the love and protection of his heart to her once again. God talks about how he'll use this betrayal to restore her. It's the story of his love for the people he called his chosen ones. But it's also a story of me and you.

Think about that for a moment with me. God says he will "allure her into the wilderness." These verses refer to the way God led the Israelites into the wilderness before taking them to the Promised Land. What did he do in the wilderness? He refined the Israelites. Loved them. Taught them. Prepared them. Disciplined them. Gave himself to them. Provided for them and became their all. All before they made it to the Promised Land.

I always thought this verse referred to God wooing Israel into a quiet place, away from the noise of the world, to speak gently and tenderly to her. I pictured Israel sitting by a cool stream with God speaking love over her, restoring all that had been lost. But I had never thought of the harder aspects of this verse. God brought Israel to the wilderness to pour his love on her, and as we know, God's love for us includes both the things we might call good and the things we might call hard, all with the greater purpose of making us more like him.

I know many of us feel like we're living in the wilderness. Certainly, my friend Lindsey felt like she was after her affair. We can see the Promised Land just ahead and wish we were already there, but the road looks long and lonely, and there are pits and giant stones to trip over along the way. If we're honest, we'll admit that sometimes it's hard to see the purpose behind why God would want us to go through the difficult places. All we know is that we just want out, just want the pain to go away, just want to lie down beside still waters and rest.

But when we see the wilderness as his tender, loving gift to us, to prepare us for what's ahead, to bless us in ways we can't even imagine, to lead us out of and away from the things that are hurting us more than helping us, then it begins to make sense...maybe even have purpose.

It took years for Lindsey to rebuild her life, but she would tell you now that the circumstances surrounding her affair were used to strip her of everything and clothe her in Christ. I count her as one of my dear friends, and I can tell you that the light of Jesus shines through her. She and her husband now help other couples struggling with their marriages to find the same hard-won freedom they've found.

When Lindsey's husband moved past his own hurt and saw hers, loving her in the midst of her sin, she never dreamed they would share their story publicly, or that God would use it to restore other marriages. But he has. He removed the vines that weren't of him, and gave them a whole vineyard in their place.

The wilderness, where God pursues us to lovingly strip, teach, and restore, is painful. But those who "come up out of the wilderness leaning upon Christ as their beloved," as Matthew Henry put it, find the true Promised Land—that Christ is our all, able to take our wrongs and make them right, able to restore us after years of hurt and bad decisions, able to give us a life we never dreamed we could have—in him.

Friend, if Jesus is wooing you to the wilderness, go. Let him remove the things from your life that are only holding you back, even if it hurts, and trust him to be kind. Your heart is what he's after, and he loves you so much that he won't rest until he has it. What a crazy, amazing kind of love.

Pray with me?

Lord, I'm afraid of the wilderness. I don't want to go if it means pain. But I do want more of you. I want to be free of all the things that hinder me so I can be more free in you. Help me take my first step of faith. In Jesus's name, amen.

Going Deeper

- Have you ever experienced the relentless love of Christ? Remind yourself now of what that time felt like for you. Was it wonderful? Hard? Life-giving? All of the above?

- Do you sense God leading you to the wilderness? Are you afraid to go? Confess that to your loving Father now and ask him to help you trust. Then go.

◇◇◇◇◇◇◇◇◇◇◇◇◇◇◇◇◇◇◇◇◇◇◇◇◇◇◇◇◇◇◇◇◇◇◇◇◇◇

Christ is able to give us
a life we never dreamed we could have
—in him.

◇◇◇◇◇◇◇◇◇◇◇◇◇◇◇◇◇◇◇◇◇◇◇◇◇◇◇◇◇◇◇◇◇◇◇◇◇◇

He Longs to Be Gracious to You

*Therefore the L*ORD *waits to be gracious to you, and therefore he exalts himself to show mercy to you. For the L*ORD *is a God of justice; blessed are all those who wait for him.*

ISAIAH 30:18

Stacey

It happens more times than I care to admit. I overestimate my own awesomeness and believe I am capable of more than I truly am. This usually happens when I need to run a quick errand and suddenly every child in my house wants to tag along. "Mommy, can I come, too?" they sing in four-part harmony when I'm trying to quietly sneak out the door. I hear myself saying, "Yes. Get your shoes," while my own inner phantom mom is telling me I am going to see the error of my ways probably in a public display. She tends to be right much of the time.

In my head I'm the mom shopping at the store with my kids all smiley and helping to put healthy items in the cart while I casually chat with a friend I bumped into. In my reality, with my inner phantom mom standing cross-armed and glaring next to the brownie mixes, my kids are doing backflips down the aisle and screaming about what a bad mom I am for not letting them get all the sugar our cart can hold. I'm having a spectacular parenting moment when I see someone I haven't run into for a while. She is perfectly dressed and of course her kids are home cleaning the house. In epic form, I fail in every way. There is no awesomeness as I assumed, and I become that mom with those kids. At this moment I think I could possibly use up all the grace God has for me for all of my years.

But there is better news for me than I can imagine: "The story of grace includes a broad range of characters—rich, poor, powerful, and powerless…For all of them, it is God's grace that tips the scale in their favor."*

His scale bends grace. He doesn't stack up my failure on one side and check to see if there is enough grace to compensate. No. His grace has already absorbed my sin. The needle swings heavy under the weight of grace. I've been released and accepted just as I am.

Sometime later I sit in my room with a cup of hot tea and think about my lack and his abundance. I plan on being here in this moment for as long as my kids will let me. I close my eyes and sink into the chair. It starts with a pinging sound. One. Then two. Now more like a trickle. Before long the gentle steadiness of the rain is all I hear. Rain is pouring down in the grayness of a Friday afternoon interrupting my quiet. I take it all in, and all at once I am covered by this unexpected symphony. It is as though it is just for me.

And I read grace. It says, "the Eternal One yearns to give you grace and *boundless* compassion; that's why He waits" (Isaiah 30:18 THE VOICE). I turn these words around and around in my head and dig

---

* Andy Stanley, *The Grace of God* (Nashville, TN: Thomas Nelson, 2011), xv.

deeper. I find that the existing One waits to ambush me with favor and tender affection. I find that this highly exalted One blesses those who long for him with the same affection.

His longing is for me—the yeller, the shamer, the if-looks-could-kill-you'd-be-in-big-trouble girl. He who sits exalted longs to shows me mercy. He waits to pour out tenderness upon me. I see it is about relationship after all. Grace makes the relationship possible. He is the one who ambushed me with grace while I was having my moment in the store with my kids. He is the one who provided the rain to wash over me the same.

And I'm undone. He has loved me first. His grace is continually tipping the scale in my favor, and the one thing he wants more than anything from me is to return the affection back to him.

Pray with me?

> Jesus, I love that you long to pour grace over my life. Thank you for loving me so much. Let this be what grounds me today. May it make a difference in how I reveal that grace to my family. Let grace rule here. In Jesus's name, amen.

Going Deeper

- Do you often feel like you have used up all the grace God has for you?

- God yearns to give you grace and boundless compassion (Isaiah 30:18). Take a moment and receive this promise by prayer. Tell him you are taking it for yourself by faith.

- What does God's scale-bending grace do in the deepest part of your heart? Do you believe it?

His longing is for you—the yeller, the shamer, the if-looks-could-kill-you'd-be-in-big-trouble girl.

He Wants to Do a Great Work in You

The Lord said to Hosea, "Go, take to yourself a wife
of whoredom and have children of whoredom, for the
land commits great whoredom by forsaking the Lord."

HOSEA 1:2-3

Brooke

Uhat? Really, God? You're serious? You want me to do *what*?"
I imagine Hosea's response to God's request of him sounded something like that, don't you? Of course, I don't know for sure. The Scriptures only tell us that Hosea obeyed, knowing that he had been called to live his life a little differently from those around him. His life had purpose in a world that was running amok, and he knew it. So our story starts with him taking a prostitute for a wife. Then having children with her. Then watching her betray him. Then taking her back.

I don't know if I could sign up for a life like that. You? If I had known on my wedding day that my husband would betray me, would I have walked down the aisle? If I had known I would lose our third baby, would I have prevented the pregnancy? If I had known loving my children would cost me so much, would I have chosen not to have them? The answers to those questions are hard, but they do make me pause and ask the question, "What is the point of my life?"

When I was younger, I just knew God was going to use me. I often sat back and dreamed about what my life would be like. I imagined it full and joyful, with the freedom to follow God wherever he led, serving him for the sake of others. And really, that is what my life is now...but it doesn't look a thing like I imagined it would all those years ago. I imagined something big; God has called me to the small, everyday task of motherhood. I thought following Christ would be the easiest decision, when in fact, it's often the hardest. I just *knew* living for Jesus meant an automatically happy, self-fulfilled, pleasurable life. Sometimes it is that, but when we open our minds to the possibility that living for Jesus means allowing him to display his splendor in our stories to those around us, it changes everything.

Hosea knew going in to his marriage that God was asking something ridiculously special of him, something humanly impossible. God had chosen Hosea's life as a canvas to display the splendor of the gospel. We can look at his life and SEE the gospel in action. Can others see it in yours?

What if our response to every single circumstance in our lives, big or small, was, "This is happening to display the glory of God in my life. It's not just for me, but so others can see him in me." What if we recognized that we've been called to live our lives a little differently from those around us, and that our stories have divine purpose in a world that's running amok?

Granted, God doesn't always tell us ahead of time what he's doing, but does he need to? We don't need a neon sign telling us he's at work around us and that our lives are designed for HIS glory and purpose, not our own. We know this life isn't about us at all.

So when "that thing" happens that we don't like, or "that thing" we've been praying for for years still hasn't happened, we have two choices. First, we can fight God, whine, and ask, "Why me?" We can allow our circumstances to define us. *Or* we can thank God for using us to display his splendor to those around us, for letting us be a part of his gospel story. We *know* he'll take care of us. We *know* he's good. We can trust what he allows (even if it hurts), knowing there's deeper meaning than what we can see. Our lives as believers are about *him*, not us. He wants to do a great work in us, and therefore our response to difficult circumstances matters.

It's a choice to either see life through our own eyes or through the bigger lens of what God is doing in the whole world.

Maybe, just maybe, God has chosen our lives to be a picture of the gospel to those around us. That gives rich and deep meaning to all the things we don't understand and helps us see that our response to them is of the utmost importance.

Pray with me?

> Lord, help me to choose to allow you to make your name great through me. Help me to see living the story you've called me to as a great and high honor, because it gives others the chance to see the depth of your great love. In Jesus's name, amen.

Going Deeper

- What are you going through right now? Take a moment to write it all down, and then stop, asking God to help you see your circumstances through the lens of his gospel story.

- What might he be trying to accomplish through your story? Who might he be trying to reach? Ask him to give you the strength to walk it out well, giving him permission to display his splendor in you.

∞∞∞∞∞∞∞∞∞∞∞∞∞∞∞∞∞∞∞∞∞∞∞∞∞

Thank God for using you to
display his splendor to those around you,
for letting you be a part of his gospel story.

∞∞∞∞∞∞∞∞∞∞∞∞∞∞∞∞∞∞∞∞∞∞∞∞∞

He Restores You

He restores my soul. He leads me in paths
of righteousness for his name's sake.

PSALM 23:3

Stacey

Gather a group of moms around a table and talk about life and pretty soon we will all be comparing notes on how tired we are. We might come to the conclusion, rightly so, that we have been tired since they handed us the baby years ago and now we wouldn't know what to do with a night of uninterrupted rest. Sleep does not seem to be part of the mothering journey. I've learned to cope and I'm sure you have to.

But what happens when your sleepless nights and grueling days turn into a weariness a nap won't fix? Do we crumble when it settles deep and hope seems to be fading? Well, that is an option, but I can tell you from past experience there is a better way. What if instead we carved out time in our crazy busy lives to actually experience daily restoration? Doesn't that sound glorious?

My friend Kristen has been teaching me about Sabbath moments. I have always struggled with the idea of a whole 24 hours for rest. As a mom, I think it might just be impossible. Kristen has given words to something I've probably known for some time.

When given a surrendered moment, Jesus can bring wholeness and healing in the midst of life pulling us in every direction. He can restore us in whatever time we wholly give to him. He can do that for us. I think he is waiting to. I love Psalm 23:3 as it is written in The Message: "True to your word, you let me catch my breath and send me in the right direction." Sabbath moments let us catch our breath and through the leading of Christ we are set right-side up.

Every bit of the restoration process is about him and the work he does in our lives. We come broken and he puts us back together. We come weary and he breathes life. We come needy and he fills us up with all we need. He revives; he resuscitates; he brings us life. I think at times we get hung up on the fact that we have exactly no substantial time to rest and be still in the presence of the Lord. We think we need large amounts of time, but what we really need is purposeful time. We need to come often and we need to come for the express purpose of being refreshed and restored.

You know, if you wear a pedometer you can actually count all your steps during the day. Those steps add up to a couple of miles of exercise, which is great for your physical health. If we can find a way to just keep walking into Sabbath moments with Jesus, they will count for our soul health as well. We just have to keep entering into those rest-filled moments, minutes, even seconds with the Lord. Maybe it is while you are doing dishes or just after you put down your kids for a nap. Maybe it is on your way to the grocery store. Weary moms need it. I know I do. But we have to fight for those moments and run to Jesus like our lives depend on it. I think they actually do.

Sweet friend, these are our busy years. We have so many people who need us to love them well. We can't put off our soul-healing restoration for a day when we have more time. We must find time to be in the unrushed presence of Jesus, even if it is only a few moments here and there.

Years ago, I went to a church where the pastor would often say, "I'm talking to you and I'm talking to me. But really, I'm talking to me first." This message, I want you to know, is for me as well. I struggle with this concept tremendously. I am a constant work-in-progress—the journey of a weary mom turning to Jesus to be restored. But I have seen small steps of progress. I know the way to wholeness starts with baby steps toward Jesus. Just because I haven't figured it all out doesn't mean I can't show you the way. It just means we can walk it together and cheer for each other on the hard days. I know today, more than any other, I need to catch my breath and be set back down in the right direction. Let's do it together.

Pray with me?

> Lord, I give you this moment as a Sabbath today. I come to you to worship at your feet. Give me rest in the midst of crazy weary days. Let me find you when I'm doing the dishes, running errands, or putting the kids to bed. Let's string together a collection of Sabbath moments that will reveal your glory, Lord. In Jesus's name, amen.

Going Deeper

- What do you think about giving Jesus the small moments in your day to meet with him purposefully?
- Do you believe he can do a restoring work in your life even if it is only five minutes?
- Are you willing to trust him with your first five minutes?

◇◇

We can't put off our soul-healing restoration for a day
when we have more time. We must find time to be in
the unrushed presence of Jesus, even if it is only a few
moments here and there.

◇◇

He Meets You in Your Mess

For out of the abundance of the heart the mouth speaks.
MATTHEW 12:34

Brooke

I was in grad school for the better part of the time my husband and I were dating. Because I'm an overachiever I took more than a full load each semester. I wasn't working, so it seemed like a good idea to give it everything I had and finish up as fast as possible. However, I quickly realized that my old organizational habits from undergrad weren't going to cut it if I wanted to survive. In order to get all my assignments done on time, I devised an elaborate system of keeping up with what I needed to be doing when.

It was an intense system—what some might call a bit anal—but it kept me sane and on top of my schedule. If I hadn't done it, I would never have made it through.

Now, one husband, two boys, and over ten years later, my husband often looks at me and says, "You know? I really thought you were going to be more organized..."

Poor guy. He thought because I was so organized while we were dating, that would somehow transfer over into our married life. Can you imagine?

From where I am right now, I can see about one hundred billion things that need to be done around my house. There are toys in the chair in my family room, a baseball bat on the couch, and a bag of picture frames on the floor beside me (because I start projects and then have a hard time finishing them). The carpet needs to be seriously deep cleaned (or ripped up altogether, because...boys and dogs...need I say more?), my bookcase needs to be cleared of Legos, there's mail on the mantle that needs to be put away, and we won't even talk about the dust situation, or what I can see in the kitchen out of the corner of my eye.

Even worse is the mess that seems to have moved into my heart. Just yesterday I told a friend, "Today was the worst day ever. What business do I have telling other moms how to choose hope when I couldn't even choose it for myself?"

Man, when I really start looking, my mess feels overwhelming. Not every day, but some days for sure.

I can't really explain why I was able to keep such a tight reign on myself back in grad school but can't seem to swing it now. The only possible reasons that make sense are the two little boys who turned my overachiever lifestyle right on its head when they were born, and haven't righted it since.

Why do children do this? I mean, I had all the answers about raising boys before I had any. I knew exactly what I was going to do, how I was going to do it, and how they were going to respond—which, of course, would be in my favor. The only problem is that none of that happened, and my ability to schedule my life, plan for it, and make things happen through sheer hard work and determination went flying out the window when they came flying in.

With each day that passes, I'm more convinced I have absolutely no power to change the hearts of my boys. Oh, I can change their behavior if I try hard enough. Anyone can do that. But I know that what's in the heart eventually comes out. I know if their knees are ever to bend to Jesus as Savior, their hearts must bend first. And that's God's business.

You might think I find this knowledge comforting, but actually, I sometimes don't. I feel most comforted when I'm the most in the control, and my boys have shown me in no uncertain terms how little control I really have. I *want* to be able to change their hearts, and the knowledge that I can't often feels overwhelming.

Some days, motherhood brings out the worst in me. But I'm learning that that's okay.

Motherhood kind of took me by surprise. You too? When my first son was born I had a terrible time nursing him, and it turned into the first of many, many things that just didn't come easily to me as a mom. I remember being so angry with God because he wouldn't change my situation and make things easier.

Angry. An ugly word, isn't it? But I found it in my heart, and as we all know by now, what's in the heart comes out of the mouth (Matthew 12:34). Oh, weary mama, I'm honestly a bit ashamed of how many times I've been angry over the last seven years of my life. On the outside, I'm a grown woman who has her life together. I have a nice house, a hunky husband, and two seriously beautiful, talented little boys. But on the inside, I'm a two-year-old stamping her foot and screaming because she can't get her own way.

All I want is for my boys to obey me. And to be quiet. And to stop wrestling all the time. And to put their toys away. And to stop goofing off at the table. And to stop spilling their drinks. And to stop wrinkling their noses at the dinners I work hard to fix for them. And to focus on their school work. And to stop fighting with each other. And to be quiet (did I already say that?). Do you find yourself nodding your head? Sighing deeply because you kinda know what I mean? We don't just have messes, we *are* messes.

Yep, motherhood brings out the very worst in me. But after seven years of battling, I've finally come to this:

I'm glad.

Lord, have mercy...what if all that junk had stayed inside of me all those years? I had no idea what a mess I was ten years ago when I was struggling through grad school. What if my inner two-year-old with cute pigtails that bounce when she stamps her foot had been allowed to grow up into an intolerable woman no one could stand?

Gives me the shivers.

I've known many women who were never called out on their inner two-year-old. It isn't pretty, so yeah, I'm saying it loud today: I'm glad my kids bring out all my ugly. I'm glad they make me disorganized. I'm glad they keep me on my knees in prayer, asking, begging God to make me more like him so I can be the kind of mom they really need.

Why? Because all this messiness has allowed me to see God at work in my life like never before. He's not like me—afraid to go in to the veggie drawer of my refrigerator for fear of what I might find. No gloves or gas mask needed for God. He just gets in the mess with us. Right there, in the midst of it all, and walks us through.

This knowledge, and the experience of it on a daily basis, makes my disorganized mess worth it.

Pray with me?

> I'm a mess, Lord. I try really hard to keep it all together, but I don't always feel like I'm doing a good job. Help me to have grace. Help me to be grace. Help me to receive grace and lavish it on those I love. In Jesus's name, amen.

Going Deeper

- How did motherhood redefine you? Name three things about yourself that have changed since becoming a mom and how these things keep you desperate for God.

- If you're an older mom whose children are grown, see if you can find a younger mom to encourage today!

∞◇◇◇◇◇◇◇◇◇◇◇◇◇◇◇◇◇◇◇◇◇◇◇◇◇◇◇◇◇◇◇◇◇◇◇◇◇∞

God gets in the mess with us. Right there, in the midst
of it all, and walks us through.

∞◇◇◇◇◇◇◇◇◇◇◇◇◇◇◇◇◇◇◇◇◇◇◇◇◇◇◇◇◇◇◇◇◇◇◇◇◇∞

He Is Enough

Let us also lay aside every weight, and sin which
clings so closely, and let us run with endurance
the race that is set before us, looking to Jesus,
the founder and perfecter of our faith.

HEBREWS 12:2

Brooke

If there's one thing I've learned in my time as a mom, it's this: I don't have what it takes.

Some days I'm better at it than others, and there are some parts of mothering I'm better at than others, but overall, deep down in my knower, I recognize that I'm not enough for the task of motherhood.

Oh sure, I can keep them alive. At least I think so...if you don't count the time my son fell ten feet from the tree in our yard, and the time I walked out of church to find my youngest doing back handsprings on the steep hill outside, and the time my oldest wrecked his bike and smacked his blond head on the pavement...just strike those out. I'm decent at sustaining them, feeding them nutritious food, and giving them a semi-clean home to grow up in. But everything it takes to raise truly good men who love and serve the Lord? To give them an extraordinary life so they can go out there and change the world?

No, I'm pretty sure I'm just not enough.

Last year in school, my boys read the story of Nate Saint. In case you aren't familiar with him, Nate was one of the four men with Jim Elliott who were killed by the Auca Indians in Ecuador after an intense effort to reach them with the gospel of Christ.

We read a lot of stories about famous missionaries that year—Amy Carmichael, George Muller, and others—and all of them inspired my boys and me to dream about the things God might call us to do for him. But Nate's life in particular also caused me to look at our ordinary, humdrum life and feel inadequate as a mom.

You might ask, "Why does a man's story make you feel inadequate?" It's a good question, and the more I think about it, the more I realize that it's because I want my boys to be like Nate Saint. Described as determined, a hard-worker, imaginative, and creative, Nate Saint spent his formative years exploring, soaring, building, and inventing. His family was able to give him room to grow and permission to spread his wings, and it served him well his entire life. Extraordinary.

I would love to be able to provide an amazing life for my boys filled with these types of adventure. I wish my husband and I could travel with them all over the world, teaching them to sacrifice and serve others. I wish we could own a farm and teach them the value of hard physical labor. I wish we had a backyard that was big enough for them to create in. I wish my husband could quit his job so we could do ministry together as a family. I wish I knew how to better show my boys what it looks like to passionately love Jesus and follow him anywhere he leads. I wish I was better at being fun so their days could be filled with more laughter. I wish I didn't get so annoyed when they want to build a fort right after I've spent the day cleaning up.

I have a vision for the kind of life I want them to have so they can have the best foundation to grow from, but day-to-day responsibilities, finances, and even personalities hold us back. On top of that, I'm human. Flawed, sinful, and incapable of stretching my days beyond 24 hours. Knowing what I want for them and not being able to get it is all the reminder I need that I'm not enough.

But God...

When I set my sights on all I can't do for my children, I get depressed and forget that God made me the perfect mom for them. In *Hope for the Weary Mom*, Stacey writes, "Runners tell me...their pace is directly influenced by where they fix their eyes." Now I'm no runner, but I do know that when I take too much notice of what's around me—my mistakes, and how ordinary I really am—my emotions get out of whack and I can't see clearly. But if I force my eyes away from what's happening around me and fix them firmly on Jesus, I can literally feel the hope pour in. This changes the pace of my heart and gives me the strength to trust that God has my mess under control.

God gave our children to us for a reason. My children have me for a mom because that's the way God planned it. I didn't get Ruby and Fred down the street to raise. I got my two rambunctious all-in or all-out boys. My boys didn't get super-wealthy parents. Instead, they got two parents who are committed to fighting for them with everything they have.

In spite of all the things I can't give them, all the ways our life together isn't really all that extraordinary, I am the perfect mom for my children. Whatever strengths and weaknesses I possess are all a part of God's plan for their lives. Maybe that's hard to take in. Maybe you just can't see how your failures as a mom could be turned into something good to benefit your children. But it's true. You weren't born to the wrong set of parents, and neither were your kids. God uses every detail of our lives to bring him glory.

As a mom, everything we do (or don't do) has the potential to be part of our children's redemption story. Every success and every mistake, every extraordinary opportunity we're able to give them, and even the ones we just can't all add up to the sum total of what God can use to accomplish his plan in their lives.

I might want my children's lives to look like that of Nate Saint, but I have to remember that God has used just as many people for his glory who came from humble beginnings as he did those who launched from the land of opportunity. Maybe more.

So friend, you're not enough. You don't have what it takes to be a great mom. If you did, you wouldn't need a Savior. But you are the perfect, right mom for your children. God chose you for them and will use your story as part of his.

You're not enough, but God is.

Pray with me?

> Lord, I confess that I sometimes want the best for my kids so much that I overlook your best for their lives. Help me today to look less at what we don't have and focus more on teaching them with what you've given. In Jesus's name, amen.

Going Deeper

- Are there areas of your family's life you're incredibly disappointed in?
- Pray and ask God to show you how he might use those areas of your greatest struggle for something good.

You're not enough, but God is.

He Is in Control

I remain confident of this: I will see the goodness
of the LORD in the land of the living.
PSALM 27:13

Brooke

Do you remember when you realized life wasn't all about you?

Man, I do. I was fresh into a new ministry job—my first "real" job while I finished grad school—a newbie in every way when it came to the nuances of the nonprofit world, and the youngest person on staff. It was a beautiful, sunny day, and I was making my way between Staunton and Waynesboro, Virginia, when my CEO called to inform me that she would not be able to make it to the Board of Directors' meeting scheduled for that afternoon. Then, in her gentle, loving and compassionate way, she told me to take her place.

I like to believe that I've grown in my speaking abilities over the years and I'm much better now at handling problems on the fly. But in that moment, friends, I was overwhelmed with fear and anxiety. My heart started racing, my hands got sweaty, and I felt like I needed to pull over so I didn't wreck the car. The glorious sunshine that just a few minutes ago made me want to roll my windows down was now giving me a headache.

I had no idea what a Board of Directors did at their monthly meeting. In fact, I was so new to my job I had never even met any of the board members yet!

The pressure to know it all and project a successful, confident image hit me like a ton of bricks. "I'm a leader in this ministry...I'm sort of supposed to know what I'm talking about, right? What if I don't look like enough of an expert and they regret hiring me?"

I have always feared being stuck in a situation where I don't know enough about the topic to discuss it intelligently. I hate feeling inadequate or ignorant. Let me know ahead of time what the topic will be and I'll spend days, if not weeks, researching until I feel confident in my ability to speak intelligently on the subject, but please don't throw me into a situation without giving me the opportunity to do some prep work!

It's an issue, I know, and I think it's spelled c-o-n-t-r-o-l.

My husband says it all the time, and I just laugh at him and shake it off, but he's right: I do like to be in control. I don't like "what if" scenarios. They make me nervous and I worry about what the outcome will be. I'm much better off if I know exactly what to expect and can have a well-thought-out plan beforehand.

Years ago I had a friend whose highly intelligent family lived to play Trivial Pursuit. You remember that game, right? Players collect plastic pieces of pie as they answer general knowledge and popular culture questions.

I hate Trivial Pursuit.

Like, really, I hate it. Never has there been another game that so adequately and completely proves my ignorance and lack of knowledge than this one. I hated it before we were friends, I loathed it while we were friends, and I still get panic attacks just thinking about it *long* after that friendship moved on.

I dreaded seeing that hateful box get packed in the car to go with us to family campouts, Christmas celebrations, birthday parties, reunions, vacations, and on and on and on. You name the occasion, it was there. As yet another opportunity for me to display my ignorance in front of the smartest people I knew found its way into the family wagon time and time again, I felt my muscles spasm and my mind freeze up, refusing to let even the most basic pieces of information (that surely *anyone* would know) come out.

And the worst part was that I couldn't even tell them how much I hated it. Their son and I were in constant competition to be the smartest (a game he won hands-down). Admit weakness? Never.

I like to make people think that I know what I'm talking about, so when my boss asked me to take her place at the Board meeting that day, I felt I'd been thrust back into one of those despised games of Trivial Pursuit, grasping for something to make me look smarter than I really was and wishing desperately I could take the path of the fool in Proverbs who looks wise just because he keeps his mouth shut!

I parked my car outside the county library where the meeting was to be held, turned off the ignition, and then just sat there. Paralyzed. Trying to gather up enough courage to go in and conduct my business. I remember it so well—the dress, the shoes, the emotions, the looming building beckoning me to my doom, and the still, small voice that whispered in my ear as I prayed. *Brooke, this isn't about you.*

For the first time in my entire life, I considered the fact that life wasn't really about me.

But isn't that where we so often get hung up?

I know I do. I *so* quickly forget that it's not about me when my needs aren't being met, when I'm placed in a difficult situation, when my children embarrass me, or when someone I love fails despite my best efforts to help them. I hear myself saying things like, "I can't believe they would treat me like that after all I've done for them," or whining, "Lord, why are you letting this happen to me? I thought you loved me!" I can even start to despair and cry out, "I'm done, Lord. I can't suffer through this anymore. There has to be something different, something better. I can't give anymore with no hope for change."

Sound familiar?

I'm willing to bet you've experienced the "it's all about me" syndrome before as well. My friend, if there was one thing I could help you understand that has the potential to transform your walk through this life, it's this: Life isn't really about you.

The only reason it's about you in any form is because our awesome God has looked down on you with love. With great and unfathomable grace, because of that love, he had mercy on you. Through his Son, he calls us to something only he can offer. And we can only receive it through submission. Submission to his plans for our life and his right to be on the throne of our hearts. It's been my experience that his plans are always worth the sacrifice.

So my tendency to want life to be "all about me" becomes a trivial pursuit.

When I fight against the Lord and focus my attention on myself instead of him and others, I'm really just trying with all of my might to hold on to something that is second rate at best and far less than what God wants to do in me, if I'll only let go.

Pray with me?

> Lord, I confess that I like to be in control of everything.
> When I'm not, I get cranky and fussy and affect everyone

around me negatively. I don't want to do that anymore.
Will you help me lay the need to control down at your
feet and never pick it up again? In Jesus's name, amen.

Going Deeper

- Ask God to show you some of the ways you tend to
  focus on yourself instead of him.

- Do you tend to love your life in an "all about me" way?
  How could this be hurting you?

◇◇◇◇◇◇◇◇◇◇◇◇◇◇◇◇◇◇◇◇◇◇◇◇◇◇◇◇◇◇◇◇◇◇◇◇◇◇◇

When you fight against the Lord and focus
your attention on yourself instead of him and others,
you're really just holding on to something that is
second rate at best and far less than what God wants
to do in you, if you'll only let go.

◇◇◇◇◇◇◇◇◇◇◇◇◇◇◇◇◇◇◇◇◇◇◇◇◇◇◇◇◇◇◇◇◇◇◇◇◇◇◇

He Covers Your Mistakes

For I know the plans I have for you, declares
the LORD, plans for welfare and not for
evil, to give you a future and a hope.

JEREMIAH 29:11

Brooke

I try really hard to be a good mom.
     I do.

But sometimes it just doesn't turn out the way I planned.

Like sports. I swore we would never allow our sons to play two sports at the same time. That's just an unnecessary stress for an already busy family, right? But here we are with my youngest son playing flag football and soccer. In my defense, we let him play both because we thought it would encourage his older brother. Weird, I know, but there's a perfectly reasonable explanation.

I missed the deadline for football. Again. For the third year in a row. It's an issue, I know. I have a problem with my e-mail inbox called "It's exploding and my eyes glaze over just looking at it," which, as you might guess, makes it hard for me to find one e-mail from our county that has the football deadlines in it. (Remembering scheduled events—where we need to be at what time—is a serious handicap for me. It's legendary among my friends, who jokingly ask each other, "What will Brooke forget next?") Nonetheless, my oldest son, who has been dying to play football for three years now, had a mental and emotional breakdown when he realized that mama had missed the deadline...again.

My youngest had already signed up for soccer, so my glaring oversight didn't really affect his emotional well-being all that much, but my oldest had failed to make the baseball travel team, and because of that failure, he was feeling the loss of football keenly.

A friend (who knows I struggle with this and sincerely wanted to help...while making fun of me) offered to let my youngest son play on the flag football team he was coaching and promised that my oldest could be the team manager.

So we said yes, thinking that having an important leadership position would at least help him feel a part of the team, and then started juggling the schedules of two different sports teams—again, something I said I would never do.

Did I mention both of my boys take fiddle lessons two hours away from our home on the day of soccer practice? Yeah, it's a crazy day. My parents usually take the boys for the four-hour round trip, leaving me with one day a week to do all my work stuff. Nice, needed, and so helpful. But it makes for a whirlwind on the return trip from fiddle and often leaves us scooting into practice at the very last second.

It was a day such as this that caused me to feel like I'd won the Worst Mom of the Year award.

Instead of a practice, the Soccer Powers That Be had planned a make-up game. I read the e-mail, made a mental note, typed it into my calendar app complete with time of arrival, picked up the team snacks, and worked on this book all day long. My husband, bless his heart, offered to go meet my parents to pick up the boys so I could have longer to write. The plan was to meet at the practice field, where I thought the make-up game would be held.

He called me on the way to ask if I was sure the game was at the practice field instead of the game field, and I confidently said "Yes!" I had read the e-mail, put the date and time in my phone, and just knew that was where it was! I was really trying my best to be on top of our schedule, but ended up making a mess out of everything.

The game wasn't at the practice field.

My husband, who arrived five minutes before me, called and said, "Brooke, this place is a ghost town. The game isn't here." After dodging a small panic attack, I was able to confirm that he was right. It was at the game field. Like always. Nothing out of the ordinary. The e-mail even said it.

We turned around and made our way to the other side of the city as quickly as we could, but because of rush-hour traffic missed the entire first half of the game. And we lost. I remember texting my friend Jamie, who, unlike me, had apparently managed to understand a simple e-mail, saying, "I feel like the worst mom ever."

When I was pregnant with my first son, I became a bit obsessive about cleaning up our lives in the nine months before I gave birth. It was like someone held up a mirror to all our ugliness and opened my eyes to our sin. I could see ick I'd never noticed before and became overwhelmed with the need to clean it up. I was convinced that all of the non-sanctified places in our lives were going to ruin our new baby, so I tried to force myself (and my poor husband) to deal with anything that needed to be "fixed" before he came.

I nearly drove my husband crazy trying to be his personal Holy Spirit. Every time we sat down together I tried to bring something to his attention that needed prayer or repentance. You can imagine how fun our time together became, right?

And I just kept on doing it until I was about nine weeks into the pregnancy.

I had gone to work as usual and began having cramps midway through the day. Scared, I called my husband and asked him to pray. He did, and then encouraged me to call my doctor to see if I needed to come in.

I waited, and waited, and waited for that return phone call from my OB, and was near frantic when it finally came several hours later. I explained that I'd been having cramps for a few hours, and expected him to tell me to come in immediately. Instead, he told me to wait it out overnight and call back if I saw any bleeding.

The hours of that day passed painfully—both in my heart and my body—and by bedtime I was struggling to maintain composure. What if there was something wrong? What if we lost this baby? Why couldn't I pray it away? Repent of something? Control it?

My husband, who was right beside me the entire time, gently placed his hands over my still flat tummy and prayed these words:

"Lord, this baby is yours. We ask you to keep him safe and be in control of anything that might be happening. Give Brooke peace and help us get through this night. Amen."

The prayer was short and very simple, but those words changed the way I looked at our baby's life and our role in it. Our baby belonged to God.

I had forgotten that God uses every detail of our lives for his glory. Every parent will make mistakes, and there will always be circumstances outside our control. Some of these will be big, others small, but every one of them has the potential to affect our kids in some way. That sounds a bit scary until you look for the grace behind it.

Your story will also be part of your children's redemption story. Think about your own redemption story. Mine is filled with spots and spaces where somebody messed up. My parents, who always tried their best for me, made bad decisions. People who loved me said hurtful things that made a mark on my heart. Kids made fun of me and said mean things.

Everyone, everywhere experiences disappointments, hurts, and challenges as they go through life. The worst tend to be the ones God uses to bring us to him. So while I might want to protect my children from every bad thing that might possibly cross their path, I have to admit the truth of this principle in my own life.

God uses our mistakes.

Whatever strengths and weaknesses we possess are all a part of God's plan for our children's lives. It's not an excuse to do the wrong thing, but it is grace for when we mess things up.

Pray with me?

> Lord, I mess things up all the time. All. The. Time. I want to be one of those moms who has it all together, and I may look like I do on the outside...but on the inside I'm struggling to make it all work. Today, help me find rest in you. Help me remember that your grace will cover over anything I might do wrong. In Jesus's name, amen.

Going Deeper

- What are some mistakes you've made with your children for which you need to accept God's grace?

- Did your own parents make mistakes? Have you forgiven them?

God uses our mistakes. Whatever strengths and weaknesses we possess are all a part of God's plan for our children's lives. It's not an excuse to do the wrong thing, but it is grace for when we mess things up.

He Sets You Free

You were ransomed from the futile ways inherited by
your forefathers, not with perishable things such as
silver or gold, but with the precious blood of Christ.
1 Peter 1:18-19

Brooke

"I think we need a new car," he said, and my stomach lurched.

I balanced our brand-new baby boy in my arms while trying to start the spaghetti sauce and surveyed my current outfit. Nowhere close to being back in my regular clothing, smaller maternity pants and old T-shirts had become my maternity leave uniform. There was no money for an in-between wardrobe, and when I did head back to work it would only be part-time. We didn't even know exactly what our budget would be in a couple of months, and so we were trying to save every penny we had as I prepared to bring in a far smaller income than I had before.

A new car seemed ridiculous.

Sure, my husband's truck didn't have much room for a car seat, but it could be done. My four-door Civic was perfect for our on-the-go days or just around town errands. I couldn't see the need, but my husband was adamant that it was time to sell his truck and get something more family-friendly.

If you knew the depth of his love and affection for this truck, you'd understand why I knew he meant business. It was a turning point for him—from young man to family man—and somehow moving from truck to SUV was the symbol of it.

It was important to him—I could see that—but I struggled to let it happen. The practical side of me wanted to dismiss what he thought was right for our family. I had all kinds of really good excuses—"Money's too tight," "We don't even know how many hours I'll be working," "Your truck is fine; let's build our savings instead"—and felt I had every right to defend them. If I had pushed him, he would've let it go. He values my opinion and usually listens to what I say. But I sensed it was deeply meaningful for him to make this change, so I chose to submit without a fight.

Well, at least without a fight on the outside. Inside, I fought an intense battle to let it go. The only man I'd ever submitted to was my father, and only then out of intense, deep-driven respect. In fact, I'd been taught to survive without a man. My father made sure I had every ability to fend for myself should the need arise, and I was constantly rubbed raw by the need to lay down my wants and desires for the higher good of the marriage.

It wasn't always easy for me to need my husband. It was harder still to yield to him when I thought there was a better way.

Submission is difficult business, whether in marriage, at work, or in the church. It never feels good to "count others more significant than yourselves" (Philippians 2:3), at least not for me. Because of our sin nature, we're prone to putting ourselves first at all times, looking out for number one. But Jesus taught us a different way...

- "Love thy neighbor" (Matthew 19:19)
- "Look to the interests of others" (Philippians 2:4)
- "The first shall be last" (Matthew 20:16)
- "Serve others" (1 Peter 4:10)
- "Submit to each other out of reverence for Christ" (Ephesians 5:21)

There's a reason Jesus was called radical. His teaching went against everything the religious leaders of the time held to be good and holy, and he revealed errors in understanding, thinking, and actions that had been present for generations. He gave us an entirely different worldview—a different lens through which to view and understand the world around us. And while we can read about it, and easily agree that it's the better way, putting it into practice can be more difficult.

This process of laying down my old habits and choosing instead to act on what I knew to be true in God's economy, was one of the hardest things for me to learn. It still is. I don't like to submit. But I've found a different way to look at the "S" word that makes that bitter pill a bit easier to swallow.

Freedom.

We all come into our relationships with Christ bound by our upbringing, culture, circumstances, and surroundings. These things affect how we see life, how we act, and even how we understand who we are. But when our hearts intersect with Jesus, things start to change.

I used to see it as a chore—this laying down of the parts and pieces of myself that don't align with the message of Jesus. Now I see that Jesus died to give me freedom from them. For indeed, embracing his Kingdom perspective brings me a freedom unlike any I've tasted before.

Freedom to love.

Freedom to serve.

Freedom to do the better thing.

In Christ, we're no longer defined or bound by the past, old ways of thinking, or even tendencies we inherited from our upbringing. We don't have to be controlled by what we've always known, how things have always been, or even how we've always thought. According to 1 Peter 1:18-19, we've been ransomed from all the things in our past that aren't of God and given the freedom to live and love like Jesus!

That's something to celebrate! I don't have to be the old me! I have the freedom to go against my natural tendencies and love others more than I love myself. Jesus bought that right for me when he took the punishment for my sin. Simply amazing.

We still have that car—the SUV my husband insisted was the right one for us—and it's been a great family car in every possible way. After all the internal turmoil I went through before we got it, I'll be sad to see it go when its time comes. Mainly because it taught me something about loving others, letting go of who I once was, and finding the freedom to embrace a better way.

Pray with me?

> Lord, I want to be free from my old habits and patterns of thinking. Please come and help me see them for what they are—rubbish, filth, unhelpful—and give me the constant desire to walk in your ways instead. In Jesus's name, amen.

Going Deeper

- What are some habits or patterns of thought you possess from your past that need to be exchanged for the Kingdom perspective of Jesus?

- Make a list now and then spend some time in prayer asking God to help you lay them down.

You don't have to be controlled by what you've always known, how things have always been, or even how you've always thought. You've been ransomed from all the things in your past that aren't of God and given the freedom to live and love like Jesus.

He Is Your Joy

Splendor and majesty are before him;
strength and joy are in his place.

1 Chronicles 16:27

Stacey

We had a busy week. We drove back and forth and back and forth some more. My girls were good sports about it, but it was wearing on us all.

We drove by the big tree at least ten times while we were busy, driving back and forth. "Can we stop and play on the tree?" they asked.

My initial response was, "No, I'm sorry, girls. There isn't time today." But then I thought better of it. "If we can get through this week, we'll stop on Saturday." They took that promise to heart and made big plans.

Saturday came and it was glorious. The Lord gave us a nearly perfect day. As we made our way to the tree, we noticed that it was dressed in pink. It was for a wedding, someone told us. The girls imagined it was for them, and of course we knew secretly it was.

The big tree did not disappoint. We climbed as high as we could on her 300 year old branches. We marveled. Joy bubbled up. Sometimes gravity got the best of us when a hand was not close by. It didn't matter. We celebrated with cherry Icees for all.

Did I mention this busy week was also a hard week? I didn't chase after God much at all. Busy has a way of shoving everything else out of its way. In fact, I had more than a few moments where I wondered how in this crazy world I was going to get through another moment. But by grace I did. I wasn't feeling the joy much at all. But then I was reminded, "Joy is not gush. Joy is not mere jolliness. Joy is perfect acquiescence—acceptance, rest—in God's will, whatever comes."*

That day I stopped at the big tree I let go of rush and rested in knowing that God would take care of all the busy my day held. I accepted that he would take care of all my undone things, and I took time to notice the little things that really were big things. Can I tell you a secret? This moment with my girls and the tree all dressed in pink...I almost missed it. I nearly drove by it again with apologies to my cuties. I was stuck in the hard times of the week with little vision to find my way out. But even on the hard days he invites us to climb trees. To pretend we are fairies or pirates. To sing songs and sneak sips of your baby girl's cherry Icee when she isn't looking. To notice what busyness keeps us from seeing. To count good and precious gifts. To look for joy.

And guess who our hearts find in the joy dwelling place?

As it turns out, the author of joy—he climbs trees too.

A joy-filled heart finds the joy giver. When I make hard stops to enjoy the life he has graciously given, I find sweet gifts that look a

* Amy Carmichael, *Gold by Moonlight* (Fort Washington, PA: CLC Publications, 1992), 74-75.

whole lot like pink scarves tied to massively old trees. I rush through life so often. He wants me to find rest and experience joy only he can give. And all of it points to him.

He is our joy.

Pray with me?

> Jesus, you are my joy. Give me hard stops today to count my blessings. Your generosity in my life is so rich I can't count every gift. But today, Lord, I will try. In Jesus's name, amen.

Going Deeper

- Do you need to make a hard stop today and count the joy God gives graciously in your life?
- How can you meet him in the joy dwelling place today?

A joy-filled heart finds the joy giver.

He Is All You Need

*My flesh and my heart may fail, but God is the
strength of my heart and my portion forever.*
PSALM 73:26

Stacey

stood at the kitchen sink once again facing a mountain of
life stacked every which way overflowing onto the counter. I
turned on the water and cupped my hands to catch the flow. It filled
up quickly and I let it run down because it felt soothing. I must have
stood there several minutes just watching the water fill and overflow
from my hands onto sticky, dirty dishes. I guess what I longed for
was that water to wash over my heart and soothe the weary from a
long week of mothering.

You see, lately I have felt like the depth of my mess is going to
flat-out swallow me whole. I'm not really talking about the dishes
either. I'm talking about the mess that lives on the inside where people can't see.

My flesh failed big time today. I yelled. I pouted. I sighed. I complained under my breath. My heart is failing me too because it just wants a café mocha plus Jesus. It wants a massage and a quiet time. It wants a good chick flick and a friend to pray for me. Of course these extras aren't bad things in and of themselves. Elisabeth Elliot once said, "If we are honest he is not all we want, but he is all we really need."* I know what I need is Jesus, but my heart seems to be trying to run to other things as well.

As I stood at the sink, God leaned in and brought words to mind to snap me back to truth that has the potential to revive my heart. "But God is the strength of my heart and my portion forever" is nothing to gloss over.

God is Elohiym, the judge who spoke the world into place and said *let there be light*. His Spirit hovered over the waters and over the formless void of the earth and created something out of nothing. *He hovers over sink waters as well and breathes life over me.*

God is the rock of my heart. He doesn't ask me to be the strong one who has it all together. *He bears the weight of that burden.*

God is my portion forever because he is continually, indefinitely enough for me. *He is an unending supply of sufficiency when all I see is lack.*

And right there in the kitchen he met me. Tears mixed in with dish soap and I found myself releasing it all. I don't know why I hang on so tightly to my failing, fallen flesh when it has a way of squeezing out the life I know I need to live. Like Paul, I am being poured out like a drink offering every day. I need to remember every drop is precious and he alone is the source. My nightly chore became a prayer bench. It can become one every day if I let it.

My need is deep. But his sufficiency is deeper. Even on the hard

---

* Elisabeth Elliot, *Keep a Quiet Heart* (Ann Arbor, MI: Servant Publications, 1995), 57.

days when I can't pour out one more drop for my family of six, God is enough.

My strength.

My portion.

Enough.

Forever.

Pray with me?

> God, the fact that you are my portion forever means you are enough for whatever my day holds. Today I don't have much in my own strength, but I'm going to use that as my cue to run to you instead. Fill me, Lord. In Jesus's name, amen.

Going Deeper

- Do you believe he is all you need?
- Can you find a prayer bench to return to each day to remind you?

God's Spirit hovered over the waters and
created something out of nothing.
He hovers over sink waters as well and
breathes life over you.

He's Not Finished with You Yet

And I am sure of this, that he who began a good work in you will bring it to completion at the day of Jesus Christ.

PHILIPPIANS 1:6

Brooke

My boys gave their hearts to Jesus when they were nine and seven years old. It came on the tail end of a very difficult season for my oldest, who was dealing with rejection from a friend he dearly loved.

It was a painful time for him, and as a mom I struggled to know how to help him through it. He has a heart a lot like mine, with a tendency to take everything personally, analyze things to death, and retreat when he's hurt.

It doesn't look like that on the outside. My hard-to-handle boy is pretty outgoing, a hugger, and will talk your ear off if you let him. But on the inside his heart breaks when someone hurts him, and I get that feeling all too well.

I have a tendency to spew. The first time it happened I was just twenty years old. After about six months of tension in a long-time friendship, I erupted like Mount Saint Helens, and the relationship never recovered. It was ugly, and I regret my response to her to this day.

Several years later, married with children, another conflict arose between me and a friend. I got hurt and spewed my feelings at her through Twitter (of all places!). Then, about a year later, it happened again. Same scenario, different person.

It doesn't happen all the time—just when I'm really stressed, or when I've let issues go too long without addressing them. But it does happen, and each time I'm left wishing I could suck those angry, emotional words right back into my heart and mouth.

It was after the final incident that I began to realize I had a pattern that needed to be addressed, so I took my raw emotions to the Lord over and over again, asking him to grow me and mature me into a woman who could control herself. I need grace to grow. Thankfully, God specializes in just that.

There are a few points I'd like for you to see from today's verse.

1. If you've put your faith in Christ, he's begun a good work in you. It may not feel like it right now. You may not be able to see the evidence of his hand at work in your life. But it's there, working to make you more like him. All of the circumstances of your life are purposed to make you pursue Jesus.

2. Don't forget the work is a "good" one. God often uses hard things to make us realize our need for him, but needing, and getting, more of Jesus is always a good thing. When you can't see the good with your own eyes, teach yourself to speak the truth, choosing to believe the Bible over what your circumstances and emotions might try to make you believe.

3. God is the one who does the good work. We sometimes feel that all the work of becoming more like Jesus rests on our shoulders, when in reality it's the other way around. When you're a Christian, the Holy Spirit lives in you, and his job is to show you the truth. Let go of the pressure to be perfect and be persuaded of God's ability to change you into the person he has planned.

4. You're not done. Obviously, I can't go through the rest of my life avoiding conflict. The answer to my tendency to spew isn't to shut people out of my life if they might cause me to snap (if that were the case, I'd have to shut out everyone!), but rather to give myself grace to learn from my mistakes, care deeply about the way I treat others (because it shows them how much I really love Jesus), and allow the Holy Spirit to work in me, convicting me of sin, and leading me to love.

The process of change takes a lifetime to complete. In fact, Matthew Henry says, "the work of grace will never be perfected till the day of Jesus Christ, the day of his appearance." That means you have your entire life to get it right.

Recently, another friend hurt my feelings. I felt betrayed, as if somehow her words represented the value our friendship had for her. I wanted to type back a shrewd answer. I wanted to be right, to show her the truth, and make her change her mind. I wanted to pound the keyboard hard, and fast, as if the weight of my fingers on my computer could convey the depth of my feelings.

But I didn't.

For the first time in my life, I removed my fingers from the keyboard, took a step back, and prayed for guidance instead. Ultimately, I let it go, believing that our friendship was worth more than agreeing or disagreeing over much of anything. I let love cover, and I walked away with a sense of control that could only come from the Lord.

Mine is a life in need of change. And that, my friends, will never change. He isn't finished with us yet, and that might be the best hope of all.

Pray with me?

> Lord, I need you to keep working in me. Thank you for offering me a kind of love that never gives up. I know you won't finish pursuing me until my life here on earth is over. Let me walk closer and closer to you all my days. In Jesus's name, amen.

Going Deeper

- Have you ever "spewed?" How did you feel afterward?
- Realizing that God isn't finished with me yet gives me grace to grow and makes me wonder if I'm extending that same grace to others as they make mistakes. Are you?

You need grace to grow.
Thankfully, God specializes in just that.

Dear Weary Mom,

Do you feel like you've come to the end of yourself? Are you waving the white flag? We know there is weariness a nap won't fix. It settles deep down in the core of who you are and weighs heavily on everything you try to do.

We understand. We are weary moms too. We want you to know two things: You are not alone, and God wants to meet you in the middle of your mess.

We would love to walk with you on this journey of motherhood. Together we can invite him into our mess, reconnect with his heart, and find hope...right now.

Love,
Stacey & Brooke

Keep reading for the first chapter of Hope for the Weary Mom

Chapter 1

When Your Weakness
Is All You Can See

Brooke

Beer and cigarettes.

Yep…you read that right. Beer and cigarettes. The phone call went something like this:

"Honey, I need you to come home now. The two-year-old is screaming because he wants to sit on my lap while I'm nursing the baby. The baby is screaming because the two-year-old keeps trying to sit on his head. When the two-year-old tries to sit on the baby's head he can't nurse. Now he won't nurse at all and is screaming his head off. The bulldog has started crying because he wants to be fed (doesn't everybody!!) and I'm going to explode within the next ten minutes if you don't COME HOME AND BRING ME BEER AND CIGARETTES RIGHT NOW!"

He brought me a Coke and dark chocolate.

Super-Sonic Weaknesses

My precious boys were born just 23 months apart. We didn't nec-essarily plan it that way, but it happened nonetheless. If you've read my book *Praying for Boys: Asking God for the Things They Need Most*, you'll know that I actually prayed and asked God to give us boys! I wanted to raise men who loved the Lord with all of their hearts, who would choose to take a stand for what's right, who would be world-changers. It had occurred to me that there was a shortage of truly godly men in the world, and that as parents, we were losing the bat-tle for the hearts of our sons. So during a time of self-righteous pride in my own ability as a mother (yes...this was *before* we had kids) I asked God to give us boys. And he indulged me.

My boys, like any number of other little boys in the world, are infatuated with being superheroes. My life as a mother of boys includes masks, swords, light sabers, and dueling bad guys to the death.

There's rarely a day that goes by in the McGlothlin Home for Boys that doesn't involve someone wearing a cape.

I love it. I hope they always want to rescue damsels in distress, bring flowers to their mommy, and fight bad guys. Pretending to rescue those who are weaker makes them feel useful and important. Running around our house with their capes flapping in the wind makes them feel strong. I believe developing these characteristics in young boys sets them up for strength, compassion, and boldness later in life. Superheroes, those found on television, in storybooks, and (the best ones!) in the Bible give my boys something to pattern their lives after. And that's very, very good.

Yes, I want to raise strong boys. But most of the time, I have to confess, I feel terribly weak.

During that first year of my little guy's life there were many nights I didn't think we were going to make it. Both of our boys are "those boys." You know, the ones who are extremely high energy, get into everything, don't take no for an answer, would rather wrestle than breathe, only have one volume (LOUD), and generally leave my husband and me completely breathless at the end of the day? Even as little guys they fought a lot, and they still bicker more often than not.

My inner voice, the one that likes to show me all my ugly, had a field day telling me I would never measure up as a mom.

Sound familiar?

The night I called my husband asking for beer and cigarettes I was in a state of panic. I'm not a beer drinker, and I only smoked a few times in college (sorry, Mom and Dad). But as I sat on my front stoop in tears that night, cell phone in hand, toddler in the Pack 'n Play, baby in the swing (and the stinking bulldog tied to the chair!), something in me snapped. After months of trying so hard to put on a brave and sure face to my friends and family, I broke down and admitted there was no way I could raise these boys by myself.

Now maybe you're stronger than I am. Maybe you're one of those moms who has it all together. Your children jump to attention at your every command, are polite to strangers, and dance a jig while they do their chores. Maybe you don't scare the neighbors by yelling, "HELP ME, JESUS!!!" at the top of your lungs multiple times a day.

But I do. And I bet if you're honest, your life isn't all peaches and cream either. (If it is, you need to be the one writing this book!)

Of course, things do change as they grow up. It's been six years since that episode on my front porch, and I don't have anyone tugging on me to nurse or trying to sit on a sibling's head anymore (okay…maybe sometimes). We lost our precious bulldog to cancer and now have two energetic lab puppies. But I still have incredibly active, highly distractible, in-your-face little boys. Sometimes I'm tempted to think I'm all alone in my walk, and those days threaten to overwhelm me. My complete inability to change their hearts of stone into hearts of flesh makes my weaknesses blaze until they're all I can see.

We moms, we think we're all alone, don't we? We think our problems are worse than everyone else's. We think our children's sinful hearts are more sinful than everyone else's. We think our weak spots have to be hidden and can't imagine telling the truth about what's happening in our hearts. Maybe it sounds a little like this...

I've dreaded this day for over a week. Cautiously, I peek my head around the corner, just barely daring to poke it inside the door, and see that my worst fears have come true. Spotted, greeted by the mother of the birthday boy, I have no time to tuck tail and run, so I muster up all the courage I have, walk in the room, and find myself face-to-face with the non-crafty mom's worst nightmare:

The crafty-mom birthday party (cue Stephen King-ish music and the obligatory don, don, doooooooonnnnnnn).

The room is one big science experiment, literally. My friend Danielle has spent weeks preparing for the little boy birthday party of the century, and it shows. Green slime taunts me. Carefully crafted explosions that make little boys squeal with delight mock me. The entire table of elements taped above a table filled with edible petri dishes stares me down and makes me want to run and hide.

I look for a means of escape, but the exits are blocked by innocent bystanders. Wait, there's an open window. If I grab the boys by the shirt collar and quietly stuff them out the window we can shimmy down the drain pipe to the playground below and no one will know we're gone. Shoot, now they're making liquid ice on the other side of the room. New plan.

Maybe I can bribe them away. That's it. I'll woo them with the promise of a trip to Dairy Queen for their favorite ice cream before the cake is served. What's that? Hot dogs? Man! Because of our new healthy eating plan they haven't had one in a month. I'll never get them away now. They're going to figure out my big secret any second now…Mama is the most un-crafty person in the world, and birthday parties stress me out like nothing else. I'd hoped they would never see "the other side." That they would never know a birthday party could be anything other than a trip to the pool with all their friends.

Busted.

I sit down in a collapsible chair, thinking about how my own birth-day party facade is collapsing bit by bit when it happens. Those big, brown eyes that make it oh-so-difficult to stay mad for long look up at me…and he says it. Oh glory, the one thing that makes me just want to end it all, give up trying, hire a professional…anything to ease this feel-ing of complete and utter failure.

"Mom, why can't our birthday parties be more like this one?"

Sigh.

Every summer the "I'm not good enough" feelings start to creep in and make me want to give up even trying to plan a good party for my boys. Thankfully, in God's great and infinite mercy, He allowed my boys' birthdays to be just three weeks apart. They've never known individual birthday parties, and I plan to ride that wave until it spits me out on the beach, ragged and torn. The fact of the matter is that I don't have a crafty bone in my body, and it never shows more than when I'm planning a birthday party.

I hate sewing.

I don't own a glue gun.

I couldn't tell you where the tape is.

Our glue sticks are all dried out.

My boys bribe the neighbor's little girl to let them use her scissors and duct tape. And I've actually considered hiring her to do craft time with my boys once a week after she gets home from school.

My lack of crafting ability has grown my stress level to epic proportions, and my feelings of guilt and utter failure have grown with it.

One recent Thanksgiving I decided to force myself out of my non-crafty comfort zone and tried to prepare a day of wonderful education and hands-on experience for my boys. As a homeschooling family, we're always looking for ways to make the calendar come alive, and it had occurred to me that my boys, then six and four, had never really learned the story of Thanksgiving. I decided it was time for that to change.

I spent hours at my local bookstore picking out just the right books to communicate the message of Thanksgiving I wanted them to remember. I scoured the Internet looking for an audio book of the story of Squanto because my oldest loves learning about Native Americans. I painstakingly cut a Thanksgiving Tree from brown craft paper and decorated its branches with colored leaves made from outlines of my precious sons' hands, each one marked with something they were thankful for that day.

It was shaping up to be a wonderful success. That Thanksgiving Tree was my crowning crafty achievement, my very heart and soul hanging there on the wall. It should have been the best Thanksgiving ever...except it wasn't.

In reality, I spent most of Thanksgiving Day sobbing—and possibly slightly hysterical—because I couldn't believe my sons could still be so selfish, ungrateful, and yes, *thankless,* after all I'd done to serve them throughout the month. They were disobedient, ugly, unkind, and downright mean all day long, and it made me feel a bit like throwing something. I mean, couldn't they see how my hands shook as I cut that craft paper into a tree? Couldn't they see the look of sheer uncrafty determination in my eyes as I traced their little hands and taped them to the wall each day?

I may have yelled. And screamed. And wept. And threatened.

And shaken with anger over their petty arguments that were making our "celebration" a smashing…well…failure. I felt beaten down by their attitudes, and at one point literally curled away from everyone in the passenger seat of our SUV in something reminiscent of the fetal position. The words going through my mind?

This will never change. I just don't have what it takes to be the mom they need. I'm a crafting failure so I must be a failure as a mom.

I should just quit trying.

Glorified Weaknesses

So be honest, mom. How many times since you brought those blue or pink bundles home from the hospital have you just wanted to quit trying? Maybe it's something much more serious than crafting that makes you want to give up. I struggle with yelling. I get angry too often. I like things to go my way, and when they don't I can make everyone in my life miserable. Your areas of weakness could be totally different, but I bet if I asked you to list them right now you could spout them off one by one. Am I right?

How many times a day do you catch yourself thinking about what a failure you are, or how your one big mess-up will probably land that little person who watches everything you do straight in the counseling chair a bit later in life? How much of your day do you spend glorifying your weaknesses (dwelling on them, allowing negative internal commentary about them to beat you down, thinking about them constantly, etc.) and wondering what will happen if everybody finds out the truth about who you *really* are?

Glorifying weaknesses—no matter how big or small—sucks our souls dry of the life-giving hope we need to just keep going.

But there is a different way. I'm convinced that the place of our greatest weakness can unleash the power of God's greatest grace. Instead of glorifying our weaknesses, letting them control our lives and break our hearts, we can learn to use them to glorify God, confessing our weaknesses and trusting him to make them into something good.

It was during a phone call with a friend that I finally decided I might not be the only one with these kinds of issues. We'd been chatting about church this and that for just a few seconds when she interrupted the conversation to tell the little voice in her home to stop what he was doing. When that same little voice turned a bit nasty and screamed, "NO I WON'T!" to his mama on the phone, a lightbulb went off in my heart, and I knew I'd met a kindred spirit...or at least another human being who knew what I was going through.

It was a profound moment for me, inspiring me to step out from behind the curtains of my life into the light. One phone call empowered me to connect with other mothers of boys and tell my ugly truth, because I suddenly knew that if I felt alone and desperate in my mothering—consumed with the way my weaknesses were affecting my boys—there had to be other moms who felt the same way. Soon after that simple phone conversation, the Lord placed a dream in my heart for what would eventually become the MOB (Mothers of Boys) Society—an online, Christian community helping mothers delight in the chaos of raising boys. A place where boy moms can feel safe, let it all hang out, and find community and help around raising these wild and crazy, beautiful and boisterous, overwhelming but amazing boys.

> The place of our greatest weakness can unleash the power of God's greatest grace.

I chose a piece of truth that can only be found in community.

I chose to fill the empty spaces of a weary mom's life with truth instead of complaining, faith instead of fretting, grace instead of comparison, and yes...coke and dark chocolate instead of beer and cigarettes.

I stopped listening to the voices that pointed out my shame and beat me down and started filling my heart with the voice of truth.

It all sounds simple when you read it now, but in reality it can take a while to make God's voice of truth the one you hear in your moments of great weakness. Second Corinthians 12:9-10, verses that have become some of the most important, inspiring truths of my life, says it this way:

> But he said to me, "My grace is sufficient for you, for my power is made perfect in weakness." Therefore I will boast all the more gladly of my weaknesses, so that the power of Christ may rest upon me. For the sake of Christ, then, I am content with weaknesses, insults, hardships, persecutions, and calamities. For when I am weak, then I am strong.

I imagine that if Jesus himself could whisper these verses into our hearts it might sound something like this:

Can you hear me, sweet one? I'm struggling hard to be heard over the condemning voices in your head, but I want you to hear the truth and embrace it. It's okay to be weak. It's okay to not know what to do or how to do it. It's okay that you don't have the answers. I do.

What's that? You're tuning in just a little now? I'll try again...It's okay to feel lost. It's okay to need help. It's okay that you're not perfect. I am!

That's better! You're the apple of my eye! My darling girl who was so valuable to me that I gave my life for you! I want to shout my love for you from the rooftops and say it's okay to fail! It's okay to get things wrong! IT'S OKAY TO BE WEAK, because in your weakness I AM strong.

If you'll let me, I will make your place of greatest weakness into my

place of greatest grace. I'll be the strength you need to keep going, the
one who meets you in your mess, the one who leads you to the next right
thing and covers over your sin with my robe of righteousness. Trust me.
Invite me in. Shut out those other voices, because I have loved you with
an everlasting love. Nothing can ever tear you away from the strength
of my love. Listen to me.

Whatever strengths and weaknesses we possess are all a part of
God's plan for our beautiful, messy lives. He uses every detail of our
mess for his greater glory, and can redeem even our deepest, darkest,
most daring mistakes until they're more beautiful than we could've
ever imagined.

My friend Jess came to Christ in her late thirties. Prior to this,
she led something of a double life—taking the moral high ground
during the day, and struggling with promiscuity, pornography, and
other sinful, damaging choices by night. At times paralyzed by
depression and anxiety, she was crumbling from the inside out.

Desperate for relief, Jess found herself in the office of a Christian
counselor. She tells her story like this: "Two things moved me forward during that time. First, the threat of being hospitalized. That
scared me to death. Second, my counselor shared Philippians 4:13
with me, which says, 'I can do all things through him who strength-
ens me.' She also prayed for me during each of our sessions. No one
had ever done that. Besides rote prayer and rosaries, I didn't know
how to pray. And to be honest, I had given up on prayer except in
times of great need when I'd simply promise God that I'd change
my lifestyle, my behavior, anything, if only he'd take away the hurt.
Medication, counseling, and clinging for dear life to the one Bible
verse I knew by heart slowly enabled me to begin moving forward.
And then God brought me my husband, Ed. I got pregnant rather
quickly and spent a lot of time in prayer. Fear of my old sinful lifestyle catching up with me somehow or affecting our child scared

me to death. I was filled with deep guilt and horrible shame. After years of actually blocking many incidents out, they came flooding back. At the time I thought it was due to all the hormones. Now I see that God wanted me to deal with them. I was driving to work one morning and, as was my habit, talking to my unborn daughter. I also liked to sing to her, so I turned on the radio. I was flipping through unfamiliar Montana radio stations when I heard Michael W. Smith's voice. I recognized it from my college days, but it was a new song. I had never heard it before.

"But the chorus suddenly blared from my not-so-loud volume setting. I heard it loud and clear. I got it. I received it. And for the first time in my entire life, I believed it. At that moment, my life changed. It was never the same. I finally knew I was forgiven. JESUS CHRIST had died for me. ME! Now, I'm able to share my testimony of amazing grace with those God puts in my life. I know that if God can redeem the worst in me, he can do it for others, too. I could never have made these changes in my life alone. So you see, it's all him. I'm thrilled to tell others about what I'm not so they can clearly see what he is."

The thing I love most about Jess's story is that last sentence. "I'm thrilled to tell others about what I'm not so they can clearly see what he is." It's what 2 Corinthians 12:9-10 calls "boasting in weakness," and it's the very best way to see God be strong in your life.

So boast, Mom. Boast in the fact that you're not good enough, not strong enough, not smart enough, *not enough* to be a good mom, and watch what God does. That's right, boast. Tell the world you don't have it all together, don't always know the right thing to do, and don't have all the answers. Admit that your kids sometimes have fistfights or shove each other off the new toy. Own up to the yelling and wiggle out of the straitjacket you've been wearing, bound up by a need to be perfect.

Refuse those voices that cry out, "Failure! Mother mess-up!" and instead take them straight to Jesus. Even if they're true—especially if they're true—take them straight to the one who loves you and invite him in, trusting him to make his strength perfect in your weakness.

Boast in your weakness, and then be truly strong.

Connect with
Stacey Thacker and Brooke McGlothlin online!

 facebook.com/29lincolnavenue
facebook.com/BrookeWrites

 @staceythacker
@BrookeWrites

 @staceythacker
@brookemcglothlin

 pinterest.com/stacey29lincoln
pinterest.com/BrookeWrites

Join the *Hope for the Weary Mom* community
by scanning the code above with your smartphone.

Stacey Thacker is a wife and the mother of four vibrant girls. Creator of the popular blog *Mothers of Daughters*, she is a writer and speaker who loves God's Word. Her passion is to connect with women and encourage them in their walks with God. You can find her blogging at staceythacker.com and hanging out on Twitter @staceythacker.

Brooke McGlothlin is cofounder of Raising Boys Ministries, where moms and dads come to discover delight in the chaos of raising boys. You can find her writing about fighting for the hearts of her sons at the *Mothers of Boys Society* blog or living a life in pursuit of messy grace at her personal blog, www.brookemcglothlin.com. A normal day finds Brooke homeschooling her two boys and falling more and more in love with the man she's had a crush on since the third grade (who just happens to be her husband).

To learn more about books by
Stacey Thacker and Brooke McGlothlin
or to read sample chapters, log on to our website:
www.harvesthousepublishers.com

HARVEST HOUSE PUBLISHERS
EUGENE, OREGON